The Perfe

Tony Castle was born in Dover in May 1938, and after attending St John's Theological College, Wonersh, Surrey, was ordained for the Roman Catholic priesthood in 1963.

His pastoral work in the inner-city parish of Nunhead, Peckham (London) led to a growing involvement with youth work of all kinds, including the founding and training of an athletic club, work against drug abuse, etc. From 1965 to 1976 he was involved in R.E. teaching, from the primary level through to sixth forms.

As a founder member of the Thamesmead Ecumenical Group Ministry on the new GLC estate next to Abbey Wood, Tony became actively involved in practical ecumenism. At the same time he originated a community development scheme by dividing the parish into lay-led pastoral areas. He left the active pastoral ministry in 1972.

In the meantime he had begun writing, and in 1974 was appointed principal editor of *Christian Celebration*, a new liturgical/pastoral journal. This was followed by a period with the publishers Mayhew-McCrimmon, and since 1978 he has been a freelance writer and editor.

Tony Castle is married, with four children, and lives in Essex.

Books by the same author
Assemble Together
Christmas in the World (*contributor*)
Hodder Book of Christian Prayers
Hodder Book of Christian Quotations
Let's Celebrate
Pastoral Care of Young People
Quotes and Anecdotes for Preachers and Teachers
Through the Year with Pope John Paul II
Tomorrow's People
Treasury of the Holy Spirit (*Editor*)
Tuesday Again
Young People's Mass Book

The Perfection of Love

*An Anthology from
the Spiritual Writers*

Selected by
TONY CASTLE

Collins
FOUNT PAPERBACKS

First published by Fount Paperbacks, London in 1986

Made and printed in Great Britain by
William Collins Sons & Co. Ltd, Glasgow

Contents

Introduction

There is a great yawning boredom at the heart of modern society. Observe the commuters on the morning train to work; watch the young mothers pushing their prams to the local clinic; see the teenagers congregating round the local bus shelter. The vacuum within so many people is experienced as an ache, an ache for an indefinable something. Vulgar commercialism plays upon it and exploits it. Daily the TV screen portrays the continual and wearying pursuit of the 'new' and the 'different'. Many of society's ills witness to the futile efforts of young and old alike to fill the emptiness. The empty space within is uniquely shaped and the only occupant that will perfectly fit and fill it, satisfying the ache, is He who is Love (1 John 4:8).

Made by love for love, only the progress from a self-centred love to outward-going love satisfies the divinely placed discontent in every person. 'Whoever remains in me, with me in him, bears fruit in plenty' (John 15:5).

I should like to make every man, woman and child whom I meet discontented with themselves, even as I am discontented with myself. I should like to awaken in them, about their physical, their intellectual, their moral condition, that divine discontent which is the parent, first of upward aspiration and then of self-control, thought, effort to fulfil that aspiration even in part. For to be discontented with the divine discontent, and to be ashamed with the noble shame, is the very germ and first upgrowth of all virtue.

Charles Kingsley

In the early '60s, like many another student, I frequented the London Folk Clubs and became aware of the LP records specially produced to introduce the novice to the intricacies of the Folk music world. These 'sampler' records provided excerpts that demonstrated the difference between Bluegrass and C & W, City Blues and Country Blues etc.

I approached the compilation of this book with two intentions. The first was to provide 'meat' for readers, like myself, who are concerned for the development of their love of God and neighbour. The second intention was to compile a sampler of the spiritual writing of our Christian heritage, for those who were interested but fearful that the spiritual writers would be too abstract and esoteric for them. The material has been drawn from over eighty writers, ancient and modern, of both the Catholic and Protestant traditions.

The Perfection of Love is, in a sense, a book without beginning or end; for while there is a discernible development through the compilation, the contents cannot always be given a definable place. For example, our need to listen to and respond to the call of Christ (placed at the beginning) requires regular attention, no matter where we are on the path to the perfection of love: our aim and end, union with the Triune God, needs to be constantly before us, but finds its place at the end of the collection. Caught as we are between 'muck and a golden crown', temptation is part of the daily struggle but finds only a limited space.

By virtue of the great dignity conferred upon us at Baptism we are not only called to work at the perfection of love but we are united to the family of God who, as a community, seek the same end. There is no place for a spiritual life that is self-regarding.

'The spiritual life' is a dangerously ambiguous term;

indeed, it would be interesting to know what meaning any one reader at the present moment is giving to these three words. Many, I am afraid, would really be found to mean 'the life of my own inside'; and a further section, to mean something very holy, difficult and peculiar – a sort of honours course in personal religion – to which they did not intend to aspire.

Both these kinds of individualist – the people who think of the spiritual life as something which is for themselves and about themselves, and the people who regard it as something which is not for themselves – seem to need a larger horizon, within which these interesting personal facts can be placed; and seen in rather truer proportion. Any spiritual view which focuses attention on ourselves, and puts the human creature with its small ideas and adventures in the centre foreground, is dangerous till we recognize its absurdity.

Evelyn Underhill
The Spiritual Life

Charles de Foucauld's words, 'One learns to love God by loving men', should always be before us summarizing Christ's own description (Matthew 25:31–46), of the last judgement and the one thing necessary, the perfection of our love.

My sincere thanks are due to Mrs Jacquie Galley for typing the manuscript.

Tony Castle

Chapter One

Christ, the Author and Model of Perfection

Christ, Author and Model

Jesus Christ has been given to us as our model and leader. He came to teach us by word and example how greatly the Father deserves to be loved, and how he wills to be loved by men. It was not only in his own name that he loved, but in ours also. He fulfilled this primary and supreme obligation first of all for himself, and then for the whole human race, as its head and model. We can only acquit ourselves of this debt after him, and can only do so worthily through him, by making his dispositions our own, in so far as we are able to do so.

God's intention, therefore, was first that we should as Christians have a share in the treasury of divine knowledge and love that he bestowed on his only Son; then, that we should make the same use as Jesus of the knowledge that we have of God, and of the charity that has been poured into our hearts by the Holy Spirit (Romans 5:5). This we do by consecrating ourselves to the Father as Jesus did, and imitating him by loving God with our whole mind, our whole heart and our whole strength. Lastly, in order that we may follow our Lord as closely as possible, we should recall how

11

he was always thinking of his Father and how all his acts were traceable to the love he bore him:

John Nicholas Grou
Meditations on the Love of God

How are we to love God whom we do not see? (John 1:18). It is true that here below the Divine light is inaccessible; but God reveals himself to us in his son Jesus (2 Corinthians 4:6). The Incarnate Word is the authentic revelation of God and of his perfections; and the love that Christ shows us is but the manifestation of the love that God has for us.

The love of God indeed is in itself incomprehensible; it is completely beyond us; it has not entered into the mind of man to conceive what God is; his perfections are not distinct from his nature; the love of God is God himself: 'God is love' (1 John 4:8).

How then shall we have a true idea of God's love? In seeing God as he manifests himself to us under a tangible form. And what is this form? It is the humanity of Jesus. Christ is God, but God revealing himself to us. The contemplation of the sacred humanity of Jesus is the surest way for arriving at the true knowledge of God. He that seeth him, seeth the Father (John 14:9); the love that the Incarnate Word shows us, reveals the Father's love towards us, for the Word and the Father are but One (John 10:30).

This order once established does not change. Christianity is the love of God manifested to the world through Christ, and all our religion ought to be resumed in contemplating this love in Christ, and in responding to the love of Christ so that we may thereby attain to God.

Columba Marmion
Christ in His Mysteries

Even if all teachers were dead and all books were burned, the holy life of Christ would still be teaching enough for us.

John Tauler

Moulded into the image of his Son (Romans 8:29). Let us gaze upon this adorable Image, remain always with his radiance, that he may impress himself upon us. Then let us do everything in the same disposition as our Holy Master.

Blessed Elizabeth of the Trinity
Spiritual Writings

The name of Jesus is both light and nourishment. Are you not strengthened in the spirit when you meditate upon it? What else enriches the mind so much as this name of Jesus? What so restores our wasted powers, strengthens the soul in virtue, inspires it to good and honourable conduct, fosters in it all pure and saintly characteristics? No book or writing has any savour for me if I read not the name of Jesus; no colloquy or sermon grips unless the name of Jesus be heard there. As honey to the taste, as melody in the ear, as songs of gladness in the heart, so is the name of Jesus. And medicine it is as well . . . Naught but the name of Jesus can restrain the impulse of anger, repress the swelling of pride, cure the wound of envy, bridle the onslaught of luxury, extinguish the flame of carnal desire – can temper avarice, and put to flight impure and ignoble thoughts. For when I name the name of Jesus, I call into mind at once a Man meek and lowly of heart, benign, pure, temperate, merciful; a Man conspicuous for every honourable and saintly quality; and also in the same Person the Almighty God – so that he both restores me to health by

13

...s example and renders me strong by his assistance. No less than this is brought to my mind by the name of Jesus whenever I hear it.

St Bernard of Clairvaux
Sermon, *On the Name of Jesus*

He became what we are that he might make us what he is.

St Athanasius of Alexandria

Never forget this: Jesus Christ, having taken our nature, has sanctified all our actions, all our feelings: his human life was like to ours, and his divine heart is the centre of every virtue. Jesus Christ exercised every form of human activity; we must not think of our Lord as living rapt in ecstasy; on the contrary, he found the motive power of his activity in the beatific vision of the perfections of his Father; he willed to glorify his Father by sanctifying in his person the forms of activity we ourselves have to exert. We pray: he passed the nights in prayer; we work: he toiled in labour till the age of thirty; we eat: he sat at table with his disciples; we suffer contradictions on the part of men: he has known them; did the Pharisees ever leave him in peace? We suffer: he has shed tears. He suffered for us, before us, both in his body and soul, as none other has ever suffered. We experience joy: his holy soul felt ineffable joy; we take rest: sleep has likewise closed his eyelids. In a word, he has done all we do. And why has he done all this? Not only to set us the example, since he is our head; but also by all these actions, to merit for us the power of sanctifying all *our* acts: to give us that grace which renders our actions pleasing to his Father. This grace unites us to him, makes us members of his body; and in order to

14

grow up in him, to attain our perfection as his members, we have but to let this grace take possession, not only of our being, but of all our activities.

Columba Marmion
Christ the Life of the Soul

If material things please you, then praise God for them, but turn back your love upon him who made them: lest in the things that please you, you displease him. If souls please you, then love them in God, because they are mutable in themselves but in him firmly established: without him they would pass and perish. Love them, I say, in him, and draw as many souls with you to him as you can, saying to them: 'Him let us love: he made these things and is not far from them.' For he did not simply make them and leave them: but as they are from him so they are in him. See where he is, wherever there is a savour of truth: he is in the most secret place of the heart, yet the heart has strayed from him. O sinners, return to your own heart and abide in him that made you. Stand with him and you shall stand, rest in him and you shall be at peace. Where are you going, to what bleak places? Where are you going? The good that you love is from him; and in so far as it is likewise *for* him it is good and lovely; but it will rightly be turned into bitterness if it is unrightly loved and he deserted by whom it is. What goal are you making for, wandering around and about by ways so hard and laborious? Rest is not where you seek it. Seek what you seek, but it is not where you seek it. You seek happiness of life in the land of death, and it is not there. For how shall there be happiness of life where there is not life?

But our Life came down to this earth and took away our death, slew death with the abundance of his own life: and he

15

thundered, calling to us to return to him into that secret place from which he came forth to us – coming first into the Virgin's womb, where humanity was wedded to him, our mortal flesh, though not ever to be mortal; and thence *like a bridegroom coming out of his bride chamber, rejoicing as a giant to run his course*. For he did not delay but rushed on, calling to us by what he said and what he did, calling to us by his death, life, descent, and ascension to return to him. And he withdrew from our eyes, that we might return to our own heart and find him.

St Augustine of Hippo
The City of God

God Alone Satisfies Us

It is beyond natural powers to love God more than anything else, yet we have a natural tendency to do so. Fruitless, you would say, for nature to incite us to a love it cannot give. No point, surely, in letting us experience thirst for a costly draught it can never provide . . .

Although this natural tendency of ours is incapable, in itself, of bringing us to the happy state of loving God as he deserves to be loved, if only we were faithful to its promptings, God's loving care would come to our aid, would lead us on. If we co-operate with the initial assistance which God will give us, his fatherly goodness will afford us even greater help, gently leading us from good to better until we achieve that perfect love to which our natural tendency incites us. For one thing is certain: God, in his loving-kindness, never refuses his helping hand, all along the way to perfection, to the man who is faithful over a very little, who does what he can.

Not for nothing, then, does a natural tendency to love God more than anything remain in our hearts. For God it is an instrument; delicately he can pick us up with it, draw us to himself – as though keeping our hearts (like little birds) on a thread, to pull them towards him whenever his mercy moves him to compassion. For us it is a token, a reminder of our first principle, our Creator; it urges us to love him, affords us a secret intimation that we are his.

St Francis of Sales
The Love of God

The Word of God is not a sounding but a piercing Word, not pronounceable by the tongue but efficacious in the mind, not sensible to the ear but fascinating to the affection. His face is not an object possessing beauty of form but rather it is the source of all beauty and all form. It is not visible to the bodily eyes, but rejoices the eyes of the heart. And it is pleasing not because of the harmony of its colour but by reason of the ardour of the love it excites.

St Bernard of Clairvaux
Sermons on the Canticles

Be without the slightest fear, our Lord who has implanted in our hearts this desire for the infinite will never abandon us. He himself desires infinitely to satisfy it. Our desire is but a mere spark from his, and it is his most vital gift to our souls. The more a soul suffers from it, the more of this gift has it received, and the greater it is. Our desires are our measure, and we are more or less what we desire. It is clear that these

17

desires are a sort of seed, which our Lord has cast into the soil
of our souls, in order that it may develop. And the same love
which has given the desire will also give the increase. It is
sufficient that he find in us good will, for that is the good soil.

A Carthusian
They Speak by Silences

What every man looks for in life is his own salvation and the
salvation of the men he lives with. By salvation I mean first of
all the full discovery of who he himself really is. Then I mean
something of the fulfilment of his own God-given powers, in
the love of others and of God. I mean also the discovery that
he cannot find himself in himself alone, but that he must find
himself in and through others. Ultimately, these propos-
itions are summed up in two lines of the Gospel: 'If any man
would save his life, he must lose it', and, 'Love one another as
I have loved you.' It is also contained in another saying from
St Paul: 'We are all members one of another.'

The salvation I speak of is not merely a subjective,
psychological thing – a self-realization in the order of nature.
It is an objective and mystical reality – the finding of
ourselves in Christ, in the Spirit or, if you prefer, in the
supernatural order. This includes and sublimates and per-
fects the natural self-realization which it to some extent
presupposes, and usually effects, and always transcends.
Therefore this discovery of ourselves is always a losing of
ourselves – a death and resurrection. 'Your life is hidden with
Christ in God.' The discovery of ourselves in God, and of
God in ourselves, by a charity that also finds all other men in
God with ourselves is, therefore, not the discovery of
ourselves but of Christ. First of all, it is the realization that 'I
live, now not I, but Christ liveth in me', and secondly it is the

penetration of that tremendous mystery which St Paul sketched out boldly – and darkly – in his great Epistles: the mystery of the recapitulation, the summing up of all in Christ. It is to see the world in Christ, its beginning and its end. To see all things coming forth from God in the *Logos* who becomes incarnate and descends into the lowest depths of his own creation and gathers all to himself in order to restore it finally to the Father at the end of time. To find 'ourselves', then, is to find not only our poor, limited, perplexed souls, but to find the power of God that raised Christ from the dead and 'built us together in him unto a habitation of God in the Spirit' (Ephesians 2:22).

Thomas Merton
No Man is an Island

The Call to Perfection

It was the voice of a child saying 'Take, read!' which at last made St Augustine cross the frontier on which he had been lingering and turned a brilliant and selfish young professor into one of the giants of the Christian Church; and a voice which seemed to him to come from the Crucifix, which literally made the young St Francis, unsettled and unsatisfied, another man than he was before. It was while St Ignatius sat by a stream and watched the running water, and while the strange old cobbler Jacob Boehme was looking at a pewter dish, that there was shown to each of them the mystery of the Nature of God. It was the sudden sight of a picture at a crucial moment of her life which revealed to St Catherine of Genoa the beauty of Holiness, and by contrast her own horribleness; and made her for the rest of her life the friend and servant of the unseen Love. All these were various glimpses of one living Perfection; and woke up the love and desire for that living perfection, latent in every human creature, which is the same thing as the love of God, and the substance of a spiritual life. A spring is touched, a Reality always there discloses itself in its awe-inspiring majesty and intimate nearness, and becomes the ruling fact of existence; continually presenting its standards, and demanding a costly response.

Evelyn Underhill
The Spiritual Life

My only task is to be what I am, a man seeking God in silence and solitude, with respect for the demands and realities of his own vocation, and fully aware that others too are seeking the truth in their own way.

Thomas Merton
Contemplation in a World
of Action

I had always wondered why it was that God has his preferences, instead of giving each soul an equal degree of grace. Why does he shower such extraordinary favours on the Saints who at one time have been his enemies, people like St Paul and St Augustine, compelling them (you might say) to accept the graces he sends them? Why do you find, in reading the lives of the Saints, that there are some of them our Lord sees fit to hold in his arms, all the way from the cradle to the grave? Never an obstacle in their path, as they make their way up to him; grace still heading them off, so that they never manage to soil the robe of baptismal innocence. And again, I used to wonder about the poor savages and people like that, who die, such numbers of them, without ever so much as hearing the name of God mentioned. But Jesus has been gracious enough to teach me a lesson about this mystery, simply by holding up to my eyes the book of nature. I realized, then, that all the flowers he has made are beautiful; the rose in its glory, the lily in its whiteness, don't rob the tiny violet of its sweet smell, or the daisy of its charming simplicity. I saw that if all these lesser blooms wanted to be roses instead, nature would lose the gaiety of her springtime dress – there would be no little flowers to make a pattern over the countryside. And so it is with the world of souls, which is his garden. He wanted to have great Saints, to be his lilies and roses, but he has made lesser Saints as well; and these lesser ones must be content to rank as daisies and violets, lying at his feet and giving pleasure to his eye like that. Perfection consists simply in doing his will, and being just what he wants us to be.

St Thérèse of Lisieux
Autobiography of a Saint

The masterpiece of visible creation, the image of God, man is the last and the supreme link in the chain of terrestrial beings, the term of the work of creation. Possessing a material body and a spiritual soul, he touches both the visible and the invisible world. Bearing in his body the likeness of inferior beings, bearing in his soul the likeness of God himself, he is placed between creation and the Creator as the meeting-place of matter and spirit, the link between heaven and earth.

But why has God created me? – All things were made for

God, therefore, I, too, am made for him, solely for him. He is alone my essential end, my total end; he is the entire reason of my existence, the sole purpose of my life. I have no other *raison d'être* than his glory. I only exist to procure this one good for him.

God's glory is the whole purpose of my life, it is my all, the whole of me; for if I do not procure it, I have no more reason for being, I am good for nothing, and am nothing.

Joseph Tissot (editor)
The Interior Life

Everything that is born of God is truly no shadowy work, but a true life work. God will not bring forth a dead fruit, a lifeless and powerless work, but a living, new man must be born from the living God.

Johann Arndt
True Christianity

'Be ye holy because I am holy.' It seems to me that this command reiterates God's will expressed on the day of creation: 'Let us make man, wearing our own image and likeness' (Genesis 1:26). His aim has always been to identify and associate those whom he creates with himself. 'You are to share the divine nature', says St Peter (2 Peter 1:4). St Paul urges us to 'Keep unshaken to the end the principle by which we are grounded in Him' (Hebrews 3:14) and, the disciple of love tells us: 'Beloved, we are sons of God even now, and what we shall be hereafter has not been made known as yet. But we know that when he comes we shall be like him; we shall see him, then, as he is. Now, a man who rests these hopes in him lives a life of holiness; He, too, is holy' (1 John 3:2–3).

To be holy as God is holy appears to be the standard he sets for the children of his love. Has not the Master said: 'You are to be perfect as your heavenly Father is perfect'? This then is what we must do to attain the perfection demanded of us by our heavenly Father. St Paul, after having mastered the divine plan, reveals this clearly to us when he writes: 'God has chosen us out, in Christ, before the foundation of the world, to be saints, to be blameless *in his sight*, for love of him' (Ephesians 1:4).

Blessed Elizabeth of the Trinity
Spiritual Writings

Every man has a vocation to *be* someone: but he must understand clearly that in order to fulfil this vocation he can only be one person: himself.

Yet baptism gives us a sacramental character, defining our vocation in a very particular way since it tells us we must become ourselves in Christ. We must achieve our identity in him, with whom we are already sacramentally identified by water and the Holy Spirit.

What does this mean? We must be ourselves by being Christ. For a man, to be is to live. A man only lives as a man when he knows and acts according to what he loves. In this way he *becomes* the truth that he loves. So we 'become' Christ by knowledge and by love.

Now there is no fulfilment of man's true vocation in the order of nature. Man was made for more truth than he can see with his own unaided intelligence, and for more love than his will alone can achieve, and for a higher moral activity than human prudence ever planned.

The prudence of the flesh is opposed to the will of God. The works of the flesh will bury us in hell. If we know and love and act only according to the flesh, that is to say, according to the impulses of our own nature, the things we do will rapidly corrupt and destroy our whole spiritual being.

In order to be what we are meant to be, we must know Christ, and love him, and do what he did. Our destiny is in our own hands, since God has placed it there and given us his grace to do the impossible. It remains for us to take up courageously and without hesitation the work he has given us, which is the task of living our own life as Christ would live it in us.

It takes intrepid courage to live according to the truth, and there is something of martyrdom in every truly Christian life, if we take martyrdom in its original sense as a 'testimony' to the truth, sealed in our own sufferings and in our blood.

Thomas Merton
No Man is an Island

Sanctity in God is therefore the love which he bears to his own supreme goodness, a love which is supremely wise and of the most absolute rectitude.

In its full perfection sanctity exists in God alone, for he alone has a perfect love of his infinite goodness. The three divine Persons possess this essential attribute but each in His own personal 'relation'.

It will always be beyond our powers of understanding to have an exact idea of divine sanctity in itself. On the other hand, when we contemplate it in Jesus, divine sanctity reveals itself to us and commands our admiration. Man recognizes it as something which is accessible, close to him.

Columba Marmion
Christ the Ideal of the Priest

When we feel within ourselves that we desire God, then God has touched the mainspring of power, and through this touch it swings beyond itself and towards God.

Theologia Germanica

Let this, brethren, be the pattern of your life, of true holy living: Dwell with Christ in that eternal homeland in both your thought and yearning.

Turn away from no service of love for Christ in this troubled pilgrimage.

Ascend to the Father by following the Lord Christ heavenward to become free, whole and alive in leisurely meditation.

Return to your brother by following Christ earthward to be torn and divided into a thousand pieces, to become all things to all men in good works.

Disdain nothing that comes from Christ, value nothing which is not for Christ.

Thirst for one thing, have but one concern where Christ is one.

Serve the many brothers in whom Christ lives manifold.

Isaac of Stella

A root set in the finest soil, in the best climate, and blessed with all that sun and air and rain can do for it, is not in so sure a way of its growth to perfection, as every man may be, whose spirit aspires after all that which God is ready and infinitely desirous to give him. For the sun meets not the springing bud that stretches towards him with half that certainty, as

God, the source of all good, communicates himself to the soul that longs to partake of him.

William Law
A Serious Call to a Devout Life

True Christians look just the same to the world as . . . the great mass of what are called respectable men . . . who in their hearts are very different; they make no great show, they go on in the same quiet ordinary way as the others, but really they are training to be saints in heaven. They do all they can to change themselves, to become like God, to obey God, to discipline themselves, to renounce the world; but they do it in secret, both because God tells them so to do and because they do not like it to be known. Moreover, there are a number of others between these two with more or less of worldliness and more or less of faith. Yet they all look about the same to common eyes, because true religion is a hidden life in the heart; and though it cannot exist without deeds, yet these are for the most part secret deeds, secret charities, secret prayers, secret self-denials, secret struggles, secret victories . . .

And yet, though we have no right to judge others, but must leave this to God, it is very certain that a really holy man, a true saint, though he looks like other men, still has a sort of secret power in him to attract others to him who are like-minded, and to influence all who have anything in them like him. And thus it often becomes a test, whether we are like-minded with the saints of God, whether they have influence over us. And though we have seldom means of knowing at the time who are God's own saints, yet after all is over we have; and then on looking back at what is past, perhaps after they are dead and gone, if we knew them, we may ask ourselves what power they had over us, whether they attracted us, influenced us, humbled us, whether they made our hearts burn within us. Alas! too often we shall find that we were close to them for a long time, had means of knowing them and knew them not, and that is a heavy condemnation on us indeed . . . The holier a man is, the less he is understood by men of the world.

John Henry Newman

It is a total misunderstanding of the Gospel to suppose that we are to seek our own satisfaction, our own perfection, and ignore the needs of the world, ignore the very purpose of the human life of Christ, it is also a total misunderstanding to suppose that we can work for the world, as Christians, and to become saints, without being identified with Christ. 'Unless the grain of wheat falling into the ground die, itself remaineth alone.' We must not wait until we are wholly transformed into Christ before attempting to share in his work in the world – if we did we should have little to offer him, most of us, when we died. It is a logical, not a temporal, order. But unless we try more and more, every day, to make our work in the world an expression of our love of God; unless we try to make every thought and desire and action more and more completely identical with the mind and will of God, our work may remain our work instead of his, and then it will be of little value, and we may even commit the blasphemy of confusing end with means, and subordinating the love of God to the love of men.

Gerald Vann
The Divine Pity

We are drawn to love, to love God and to love perfection, and to have no reserves with God. As to whether we shall be saints or not our mind never rests on the subject. We should fling the thought off from us as a miserable temptation. All we see clearly before us is the resolution to have no reserves with God, and then to leave all else to him.

Frederick William Faber
Growth in Holiness

Chapter Two

The Work of the Spirit

Knowing the Unknowable

A good many men, Christian or otherwise, whose spirit has been marked by a certain philosophy and by the modern scientific disciplines, declare that they can no longer accept the concept of God as the Church propounds it. They consider it indispensable to strip away everything that the human spirit would have projected onto it from itself; they go so far as to speak of *idols*. Others go even so far as to assert that we can neither say nor know anything about God. Now in so far as this pressing demand for progress and purification in the knowledge of God is legitimate and possible, we must recognize that the contemplatives who have known how to translate their experience of the divine into human language give us the highest and purest expression of God that can be. We need only read the greatest among them, St John of the Cross for example, to realize this. No, God is not unknowable by the mind, but he is unutterable, which is not the same thing. The language of the mystics cannot meet the language of science or reason of course, but nevertheless in a world that craves experiential testimonies it will always be one of the roads by which our contemporaries can find God.

René Voillaume
Contemplation in the Church of Our Time

God in his one and simple essence is all the power and majesty of his attributes. He is omnipotent, wise, good, merciful, just, strong, loving; he is all the other attributes and perfections of which we have no knowledge here below. He is all this. When the soul is in union with him, and he is pleased to admit it to a special knowledge of himself, it sees all these perfections and majesty together in him . . . and as each one of these attributes is the very being of God, who is the Father, the Son and the Holy Ghost; and as each attribute is God himself; and as God is infinite light, and infinite divine fire, it follows that each attribute gives light and burns as God himself.

St John of the Cross
Living Flame of Love

O stupendous prodigy, of an incomprehensible God, who works and yet is mysteriously incomprehensible! A man bears consciously in himself God as light, him who has produced and created all things, holding even the man who carries him. Man carries him interiorly as a treasure which transcends words, written or spoken, any quality, quantity, image matter and figure, shaped in an inexplicable beauty, all entirely simple as light, he who transcends all light.

St Symeon the New Theologian

Think'st thou in temporal speech God's
  Name may uttered be?
It is unspeakable to all eternity.

Angelus Silesius
The Spiritual Maxims of
Angelus Silesius

God is unwearied patience, a meekness that cannot be provoked; he is an ever enduring mercifulness; he is unwearied goodness, impartial, universal love: he does everything that is good, righteous and lovely for its own sake, because it is good, righteous and lovely. He is the good from which nothing but good comes and resisteth all evil only with goodness. This is the nature and spirit of God.

William Law
A Serious Call to a Devout Life

But what do I love when I love Thee? Not grace of bodies, nor the beauty of the seasons, nor the brightness of the light . . . nor inexhaustible melodies of sweet song, nor the fragrant smell of flowers, of ointments and spices . . . None of these love I when I love my God: and yet I love a kind of light, and of melody and of fragrance . . . when I love my God . . .

And what is this? I asked the earth and it said, 'I am not he,' and whatsoever is in it confessed the same. I asked the sea and the deeps, and all that swimming or creeping live therein, and they answered, 'We are not thy God, seek above us.' I asked the wandering winds; and the whole air with his inhabitants spoke . . . 'I am not God.' I asked the heavens, sun, moon and stars, 'Nor [say they] are we the God whom thou seekest.' And I replied unto all those things which encompass the door of my flesh, 'Ye have told me of my God, that ye are not he: tell me something of him.' And they cried all with a great voice, 'He made us.' My questioning them was my mind's desire, and their beauty was their answer.

St Augustine of Hippo
Confessions

31

THE PERFECTION OF LOVE
Creation – the Beauty of Holiness

When I heard the learn'd astronomer,
When the proofs, the figures, were ranged in columns
    before me,
When I was shown the charts and diagrams, to add, divide
    and measure them,
When I was sitting I heard the astronomer when he
    lectured with much applause in the lecture-room,
How soon unaccountable I became tired and sick,
Till rising and gliding out I wander'd off by myself,
In the mystical moist night-air, and from time to time,
Look'd up in perfect silence at the stars.

Walt Whitman
When I Heard the Learn'd Astronomer

The imagery of the heavens as being two thousand million
light-years in diameter is awesome when compared to the
tiny earth, but trivial when compared to the imagery of the
'hand that measured the heavens'.

Fulton J. Sheen
Old Errors and New Labels

Your enjoyment of the world is never right, till every
morning you awake in heaven; see yourself in your Father's
Palace, and look upon the skies, the earth and the air as
Celestial Joys: having such a reverend esteem of all as if you
were among the angels.

You never enjoy the world aright, till the sea itself floweth
in your veins, till you are clothed with the heavens, and
crowned with the stars: and perceive yourself to be the sole

heir of the whole world, and more than so, because men are in it who are every one sole heirs as well as you. Till you can sing and rejoice and delight in God, as misers do in gold, and Kings in sceptres, you never enjoy the world . . .

The world is a mirror of infinite beauty, yet no man sees it. It is a temple of Majesty, yet no man regards it. It is the region of Light and Peace, did not men disquiet it. It is the Paradise of God.

Thomas Traherne
Centuries of Meditation

The world is God's book, which he set man at first to read; and every creature is a letter, or syllable, or word, or sentence, more or less, declaring the name and will of God.

Richard Baxter
Christian Directory

So many Christians are like deaf people at a concert. They study the programme carefully, believe every statement made in it, speak respectfully of the quality of the music, but only really hear a phrase now and again. So they have no notion at all of the mighty symphony which fills the universe, to which our lives are destined to make their tiny contribution, and which is the self-expression of the Eternal God.

Yet there are plenty of things in our normal experience, which imply the existence of that world, that music, that life. If, for instance, we consider the fact of prayer, the almost universal impulse to seek and appeal to a power beyond ourselves, and notice the heights to which it can rise in those who give themselves to it with courage and love – the power it exerts, the heroic vocations and costly sacrifices which it supports, the transformations of character which it effects – it is a sufficiently mysterious characteristic, another beauty beyond sense. And again, any mature person looking back on their own past life, will be forced to recognize factors in that life, which cannot be attributed to heredity, environment, opportunity, personal initiative or mere chance. The contact which proved decisive, the path unexpectedly opened, the other path closed, the thing we felt compelled to say, the letter we felt compelled to write. It is as if a hidden directive power, personal, living, free, were working through circumstances and often against our intention or desire; pressing us in a certain direction, and moulding us to a certain design.

All this, of course, is quite inexplicable from the materialistic standpoint. If it is true, it implies that beneath the surface of life, which generally contents us, there are unsuspected deeps and great spiritual forces which condition and control our small lives. Some people are, or become, sensitive to the pressure of these forces. The rest of us easily ignore the evidence for this whole realm of experience, just because it is all so hidden and interior; and we are so busy responding to obvious and outward things. But no psychology which fails to take account of it can claim to be complete. When we take it seriously, it surely suggests that we are essentially spiritual as well as natural creatures; and that therefore life in its fulness, the life which shall develop and use all our capabilities and fulfil all our possibilities, must involve correspondence not only with our visible and ever-changing but also with our invisible and unchanging environment: the Spirit of all spirits, God, in whom we live and move and have our being.

Evelyn Underhill
The Spiritual Life

God passes through the thicket of the world, and wherever his glance falls he turns all things to beauty.

St John of the Cross
The Spiritual Canticle

I cast my eyes back to Andromeda. The night was so clear that I could just discern the nebula that bears the name of the constellation. It is the celestial body which is farthest from the Earth yet visible to the naked eye: eight hundred thousand light years away. Between them and the Earth is Proxima, the four light years of which would appear to me in two months' time in the constellation of Centaurus. Such is the space occupied by this mass of forty million stars in which is gathered the galaxy to which we belong – on a tiny grain of sand called Earth.

Beyond the nebula Andromeda are other millions of nebulae, and thousands and thousands of stars which my eyes cannot see, but which God has created.

It is true that Jesus said, 'Go, and make disciples of all nations.' But he also added, 'Without me you can do nothing.' It is true that St Ignatius said, 'Act as though everything depended upon you.' But he added, 'But pray as though everything depended upon God.' God is the creator of the physical cosmos as well as of the human cosmos. He rules the stars as he rules the Church. And if, in his love, he has wished to make men his collaborators in the work of salvation, the limit of their power is very small and clearly defined. It is the limit of the wire compared with the electric current.

We are the wire, God is the current. Our only power is to let the current pass through us. Of course, we have the power to interrupt it and say 'no'. But nothing more . . . But the wire is one thing, the current is another. They are quite different, and there is certainly no reason for the wire to become self-satisfied, even one which transmits at high tension.

Carlo Carretto
Letters from the Desert

To know that Love alone was the beginning of nature and creature, that nothing but Love encompasses the whole universe of things, that the governing hand that overrules all, the watchful eye that sees through all, is nothing but omnipotent and omniscient Love, using an infinity of wisdom, to save every misguided creature from the miserable works of his own hands, and make happiness and glory the perpetual inheritance of all the creation, is a reflection that must be quite ravishing to every intelligent creature that is sensible of it.

William Law
A Serious Call to a Devout Life

The Gifts of the Spirit

Most of our conflicts and difficulties come from trying to deal with the spiritual and practical aspects of our life separately instead of realizing them as parts of one whole. If our practical life is centred on our own interests, cluttered up by possessions, distracted by ambitions, passions, wants and worries, beset by a sense of our own rights and importance, or anxieties for our own future or longings for our own success, we need not expect that our spiritual life will be a contrast to all this. The soul's house is not built on such a convenient plan: there are few soundproof partitions in it. Only when the conviction – not merely the idea – that the demand of the Spirit, however inconvenient, comes first and IS first, rules the whole of it, will those objectionable noises die down which have a way of penetrating into the nicely furnished little oratory, and drowning all the quieter voices by their din.

St John of the Cross, in a famous and beautiful poem, described the beginning of the journey of his soul to God:

> In an obscure night
> Fevered by Love's anxiety
> O hapless, happy plight
> I went, none seeing me,
> Forth from my house, where all things
> quiet be.

Not many of us could say that. Yet there is no real occasion for tumult, strain, conflict, anxiety, once we have reached the living conviction that God is All. All takes place within him, he alone matters, he alone is. Our spiritual life is his affair; because, whatever we may think to the contrary, it is really produced by his steady attraction, and our humble and self-forgetful response to it. It consists in being drawn, at his pace and in his way, to the place where he wants us to be; not the place we fancied ourselves.

Evelyn Underhill
The Spiritual Life

The inward stirring and touching of God makes us hungry and yearning; for the Spirit of God hunts our spirit; and the more it touches it, the greater our hunger and craving.

Jan van Ruysbroeck
The Mirror of Eternal Salvation

The Holy Spirit, who dwells in us, means to render our souls supple, pliable and obedient to his divine impulses, his heavenly inspirations. These are the laws of his love; in their observance lies the supernatural happiness of this life. So he gives us seven supernatural habits or perfections. They are called by holy Scripture (Isaiah 11:2, Acts 2:38) and in theological books, gifts of the Holy Spirit. Now, not only are they inseperable from charity, but (all things considered and strictly speaking) they are charity's chief virtues, habits, dispositions.

Wisdom, for instance, is simply the love which tastes and savours the experience of how kind, how good God is; *understanding* is simply love intent on studying, on grasping the beauty of the truths of faith – to know God in himself, first of all, and then to see him in his creatures; *knowledge*, on the contrary, is simply that same love keeping us intent on knowing ourselves and creatures, so as to lift our minds to a more perfect knowledge of the service we owe to God; *counsel* is also a love which makes us careful, anxious and capable of choosing just those things that will enable us to serve God holily; *fortitude* is love which encourages and puts new life into our hearts, so that we may carry out what counsel has decided should be done; *piety* is the love which tempers toil, which moves us to do whatever pleases God, our Father, and moves us to do it wholeheartedly, lovingly, with filial devotion; *fear*, in conclusion, is simply love that impels us to flee or avoid whatever is displeasing to God.

Thus charity becomes for us another Jacob's ladder, its steps the seven gifts of the Holy Spirit for angelic men to climb up from earth to heaven, to union with the heart of God almighty, and to come down from heaven to earth to take their neighbour by the hand, to lead him to heaven.

St Francis of Sales
The Love of God

Earthly language is entirely insufficient to describe what there is of joy, happiness, and loveliness contained in the inner wonders of God.

Jacob Boehme
The Threefold Life of Man

Faith fills a man with love for the beauty of its truth, with faith in the truth of its beauty.

St Francis of Sales
The Love of God

By his gift of faith God comes into our souls, talks to our minds. He speaks, not by words, but by inspirations. So attractively does he set the truths of faith before our minds, our wills are greatly gratified – to such an extent that the will urges the intellect to assent, to submit to the truth undoubtingly, in utter trustfulness.

There you have the wonder of it: God proposes these truths to our minds in darkness, in obscurity; we cannot clearly see them, we can only catch glimpses of them. The same sort of thing happens sometimes in the world around us when it is misty. We cannot see the sun, only a faint lightening of the sky shows where it is. We catch sight of it without seeing it, you might say; we don't see the sun well enough to say that we really do see it, yet we see enough to make it impossible for us to say that we cannot see it at all. We caught a glimpse of it, we say. Once this divine brightness of faith dawns upon the mind, it compels the obedience of the intellect without any force of reasoning or show of argument, simply by the charm of its presence. So authoritatively does it compel belief, it gives us a certitude of truth which far exceeds any certitudes on earth. It shows itself so superior to intellect or reasoning, their authority pales by comparison.

St Francis of Sales
The Love of God

That man is perfect in faith who can come to God in the utter dearth of his feelings and desires, without a glow or an aspiration, with the weight of low thoughts, failures, neglects and wandering forgetfulness and say to him, 'Thou art my refuge'.

George MacDonald
Unspoken Sermons

Given a thorough-going faith and love for Jesus Christ, there is nothing at all that will not be obvious to you; for life begins and ends with those two qualities. Faith is the beginning, and love is the end; and the union of the two together is God.

St Ignatius of Antioch
Letter to the Ephesians

Joy is the sentiment that is born in a soul, conscious of the good it possesses.

Columba Marmion
Christ in His Mysteries

We are all strings in the concert of his joy; the spirit from his mouth strikes the note and tune of our strings.

Jacob Boehme
The Threefold Life of Man

First keep thyself in peace and then shalt thou be able to pacify others. A peaceable man doth more good than he that is well learned . . . He that is well in peace is not suspicious of any. But he that is discontented and troubled is tossed with divers suspicions: he is neither quiet himself nor suffereth others to be quiet . . . He considereth what others are bound to do, and neglecteth that which he is bound to do himself. First therefore have a careful zeal over thyself, and then thou mayest justly show thyself zealous also of thy neighbour's good.

Thou knowest well how to excuse and colour thine own deeds, but thou art not willing to receive the excuses of others. It were more just that thou shouldest accuse thyself and excuse thy brother . . . It is no great matter to associate with the good and gentle; for this is naturally pleasing to all, and everyone willingly enjoyeth peace and loveth those best that agree with him. But to be able to live peaceably with hard and perverse persons, or with the disorderly or with such as go contrary to us, is a great grace, and a most commendable and manly thing.

Thomas à Kempis
The Imitation of Christ

'Take no thought for the morrow' is a heavenly maxim quite as applicable to our interior conduct, as to our exterior. Peace of heart is gained by it; for it is the most perfect remedy for all those things which disturb interior peace, which are chiefly precipitation, agitation and outward disasters. It checks precipitation, calms agitation and often prevents or mitigates the outward disasters.

Frederick William Faber
Growth in Holiness

All our goodness is a loan; God is the owner. God works and his work is God.

St John of the Cross

To be patient with self is an almost incalculable blessing, and the shortest road to improvement, as well as the quickest means by which an interior spirit can be formed within us, short of that immediate touch of God which makes some souls interior all at once. It breeds considerateness and softness of manner toward others. It disinclines us to censoriousness, because of the abiding sense of our own imperfections. It quickens our perception of utterest dependence on God and grace, and produces at the same time evenness of temper and equality of spirits, because it is at once an effort, and yet a quiet sustained effort. It is a constant source of acts of the most genuine humility. In a word, by it we act upon self from without, as if we were not self; but self's master, or self's guardian angel. When this is done in the exterior of life as well as the interior, what remains in order to perfection?

Frederick William Faber
Growth in Holiness

We come down from these heights to consider what this complete self-giving to the Spirit can mean in our own quite ordinary lives. St John of the Cross says that every quality or virtue which that Spirit really produces in men's souls has three distinguishing characters – Tranquillity, Gentleness, Strength. All our action – and now we are thinking specially of action – must be peaceful, gentle and strong. That suggests, doesn't it, an immense depth, and an invulnerable steadiness as the soul's abiding temper; a depth and a steadiness which come from the fact that our small action is now part of the total action of God, whose Spirit, as another saint has said, 'Works always in tranquillity.' Fuss and feverishness, anxiety, intensity, intolerance, instability, pessimism and wobble, and every kind of hurry and worry – even these on the highest levels, are signs of the self-made and self-acting soul; the spiritual parvenu. The saints are never like that. They share the quiet and noble qualities of the great family to which they belong; the family of the Sons of God.

If, then, we desire a simple test of the quality of our spiritual life, a consideration of the tranquillity, gentleness and strength with which we deal with the circumstances of our outward life will serve us better than anything that is based on the loftiness of our religious notions, or fervour of our religious feelings. It is a test that can be applied anywhere and at any time. Tranquillity, gentleness and strength, carrying us through the changes of weather, the ups and downs of the route, the varied surface of the road; the inequalities of family life, emotional and professional disappointments, the sudden intervention of bad fortune or bad health, the rising and falling of our religious temperature. This is the threefold imprint of the Spirit on the souls surrendered to his great action.

Evelyn Underhill
The Spiritual Life

Just as one who wheels a barrow does not employ it for his delight but only because it is useful, so the gifts of God should be nothing but useful to us, and we should take delight in God alone.

John Tauler

At each moment of time in the fullest meaning of the word *now* Christ is born in us and the Holy Ghost proceeds, bearing all its gifts. May we offer to the adornment of these gifts of the Holy Ghost the likeness of him in ourselves, but to his divinely regenerating power may we offer the sacred unity of our essence.

Jan van Ruysbroeck
*Essays on the Bases of
the Mystic Knowledge*

Chapter Three

The Primacy of Love

The Primacy of Love

Love is like the hook on a fisherman's line; the fish must take the hook or the fisherman can never catch him. After the hook is once in his mouth, the fish may swim about and even swim away from the shore, but the fisherman is sure to finally land him. And this I compare with love. Whoever is caught by love is held perfectly fast, and yet in a sweet captivity. Whoever has received the gift of Divine love, obtains from it more freedom from base natural tendencies than by practising all possible penances and austerities. He it is that can most sweetly endure all misfortunes that happen to him or threaten to overwhelm him; he is the one who most readily forgives all the injuries that can be inflicted on him. Nothing brings thee nearer to God; nothing makes God so much thy own, as the sweet bond of love. Whosoever has found this way never seeks any other. Whosoever is caught by this hook is so entirely captive, that feet, hands, mouth, eyes and heart – everything that is himself – becomes God's own. Therefore, if thou wouldst conquer these enemies, namely, corrupt natural tendencies, and render them harmless, love is thy best weapon. Therefore, it is written: 'Love is strong as death, (its) jealousy hard as hell' (Cant.viii,6). Death cuts the soul from the body, but love cuts all things from the soul. When the soul loves, then whatsoever is not God or Godlike, it suffers not to rest with it for an instant. Whosoever is enlisted in this warfare and treads this path, what he does or what he does not in active good works, or what he is not able to do, makes no difference – whether something or nothing, all is for love. The work of perfect love is more fruitful to a man's own soul and to the souls of all other men with whom he deals, and it brings more glory to God, than all other works, even if these be free from mortal sin, but are done in a state of weaker love. The mere quiet repose of a soul with perfect love, is of more worth to God and man than the active labours of another soul. Therefore, do thou but cleave fast and firm to this hook of Divine love and thou shalt be God's happy captive, and the more entirely captive, the more perfectly free shalt thou be.

John Tauler
The Sermons and Conferences
of John Tauler

The freedom that is in our nature is our ability to love something, someone besides ourselves, and for the sake, not of ourselves, but of the one we love. There is in the human will an innate tendency, an inborn capacity for disinterested love. This power to love another for his own sake is one of the things that makes us like God, because this power is the one thing in us that is free from all determination. It is a power which transcends and escapes the inevitability of self-love.

Thomas Merton
From unpublished notes in
Merton at Prayer

If mountains can be moved by faith, is there less power in love?

Frederick William Faber
Sermons

46

A great thing is love, a great good every way; which alone lightens every burden and bears equally every inequality.

For it carries a burden without being burdened, and makes every bitter thing sweet and savoury.

The noble love of Jesus impels a man to do great things, and ever excites him to desire that which is more perfect.

Love wills to be free and to be detached from all worldly affection, so that its inward vision be not hindered, and that it suffer no entanglement in temporal prosperity, or discomfiture of misfortune.

Nothing is sweeter than love, nothing stronger, nothing higher, nothing wider, nothing more pleasant, nothing fuller or better in heaven or in earth; for love is born of God, and cannot rest but in God, above all created things.

The lover flies, runs and rejoices; he is free and is not bound.

He gives all for all, and has all in all; because he rests above all created things in the one Sovereign Being, from whom flows and proceeds every thing that is good.

He does not regard the gifts, but transcending all good things betakes himself to the giver.

Love often knows no measure, but grows fervent beyond all measure.

Love feels no burden, thinks lightly of labours, aims beyond its strength, complains not of impossibility; for it conceives that all things are possible to it, and all things free.

Love, therefore, is equal to any task; and it often fulfils and succeeds, when he that does not love faints and lies prostrate.

Love keeps watch, and sleeping slumbers not.

Though wearied, it is not worn out; though straitened, it is not constrained; though disturbed, it is not alarmed; but, like a living flame and burning torch, it forces its way upwards and safely passes through.

If any man loves, he knows what this voice cries.

For that ardent affection of the soul is a great cry in the ears of God, and this is what it says: My God and my Love! Thou art all mine and I am all Thine.

Enlarge me in love, that I may learn to taste with the inward palate of my heart how sweet it is to love, and to melt and bathe in love.

Let me be possessed by love and mount above myself from very fervour and ecstasy of love.

Let me sing love's song; let me follow Thee, my Beloved, to the heights; let my soul quite lose itself in Thy praises, rejoicing exceedingly in love.

Let me love Thee more than myself, and myself only for Thee. And in Thee let me love all who truly love Thee, as is commanded by the law of love which shines forth from Thee.

Love is swift, sincere, devoted, cheerful and delightful; strong, patient, faithful, prudent, long-suffering, manly, and never self-seeking.

For when a man seeks himself, then he falls from love.

Love is circumspect, humble, upright; not soft, nor fickle, nor intent upon vain things. It is sober, chaste, steadfast, quiet, and keeps guard over all the senses.

Love is submissive and obedient to superiors; in its own eyes mean and contemptible, towards God devout and thankful; always trusting and hoping in him, even when it does not taste the savour of God's sweetness; for there is no living in love without some sorrow.

Whosoever is not ready to suffer all things, and to stand resigned to the will of his Beloved, he is not worthy to be called a lover.

A lover must willingly embrace all that is hard and bitter for the sake of his Beloved, and never suffer himself to be turned away from him by any obstacle whatsoever.

Thomas à Kempis
The Imitation of Christ

Love goes into God's presence unannounced,
    while at the gate
Reason and Knowledge must remain,
    and for an audience wait.

Angelus Silesius
*The Spiritual Maxims
of Angelus Silesius*

You are as prone to love, as the sun is to shine; it being the most delightful and natural employment of the soul of man: without which you are dark and miserable. Consider then the extent of love, its vigour and excellency, for certainly he that delights not in love makes vain the universe, and is of necessity to himself the greatest burden. The whole world ministers to you as the theatre of your love. It sustains you and all objects that you may continue to love them.

Thomas Traherne
Centuries of Meditations

Now mayest thou ask me and say: Thou speakest so much of love; tell me what love is, and where it is, and how I shall love God truly. The first asking is: What is love? and I answer, love is a burning yearning in God, with a wonderful delight and secureness. God is light and burning. Light clarifies our skill, burning kindles our longings, that we may desire naught but Him. Love is the desire of the heart, aye thinking on that it loves; and when it has that it loves, then it joys, and nothing may make it sorry. The other asking is: Where is love? And I answer, love is in the heart and in the will of man, not in his work, but in his soul. For many speak good and do good, and love not God: as hypocrites which suffer great penance and seem holy in men's sight. But for that they seek loving and honour of men, and favour, they have lost their reward, and in the sight of God are the devil's sons, and ravishing wolves. The third asking is: How shall I truly love God? I answer: My love is, to love him in all thy might stalwartly; in all thy heart wisely; in all thy soul devoutly and sweetly. Stalwartly may no man love him but if he be stalwart. He is stalwart that is meek: for all spiritual strength comes of meekness – on whom rests the Holy Ghost? In a meek soul. Meekness governs us and keeps us in all our temptations, so that they overcome us not. Proud men and women love not stalwartly: for they are so weak that they fall at every stirring of the wind, that is temptation. In nothing may men sooner overcome the devil, than in meekness, that he greatly hates. Also it behoves thee to love God wisely; and that may thou not do but if thou be wise. Thou art wise when thou art poor, without desire of this world, and despisest thyself for the love of Jesus Christ; and expendest all thy wit and all thy might in his service. Whoso will love wisely, it behoves him to love lasting things lastingly, and passing things passingly; so that his heart be set and fastened on nothing but in God.

Richard Rolle
The Fire of Love

I was being tormented by this question of unfulfilled longings and it was a real martyrdom in my prayer, when I decided to consult St Paul's epistles in the hopes of getting an answer. It was the twelfth and thirteenth chapters of First Corinthians that claimed my attention. The first of these told me that we can't all of us be apostles, all of us be prophets, all of us doctors, and so on; the Church is composed of members which differ in their use; the eye is one thing and the hand is another. It was a clear enough answer, but it didn't satisfy my aspirations, didn't set my heart at rest. The Magdalen, by stooping now and again into the empty tomb, was at last rewarded for her search; and I, by sinking down into the depths of my own nothingness, rose high enough to find what I wanted! Reading on to the end of the chapter, I met this comforting phrase: 'Prize the best gifts of heaven. Meanwhile, I can show you a way which is better than any other.'

What was it? The Apostle goes on to explain that all the gifts of heaven, even the most perfect of them, without love, are absolutely nothing; charity is the best way of all, because it leads straight to God. Now I was at peace; when St Paul was talking about the different members of the Mystical Body I couldn't recognize myself in any of them; or rather I could recognize myself in all of them. But charity – that was the key to my vocation. If the Church was a body composed of different members, it couldn't lack the noblest of all; it must have a heart, and a heart burning with love. And I realized that this love was the true motive force which enabled the other members of the Church to act; if it ceased to function the Apostle would forget to preach the Gospel, the Martyrs would refuse to shed their blood. Love, in fact, is the vocation which includes all others; it's a universe of its own, comprising all time and space – it's eternal. Beside myself with joy, I cried out: 'Jesus, my Love! I've found my vocation, and my vocation is love.' I had discovered where it is that I belong in the Church, the place God has appointed for me. To be nothing else than love, deep down in the heart of Mother Church; that's to be everything at once – my dream wasn't a dream after all.

St Thérèse of Lisieux
Autobiography of a Saint

Love is no longer a tendency of him who loves; it is a loving intimacy, which establishes the spiritual man in the unity of faith, without his having any further need of time nor of space. Already established by love in the good things that he will possess, having anticipated hope by spiritual knowledge, he no longer tends toward anything, having everything that he could tend toward. He remains, then, in the one unchanging attitude, loving in a spiritual fashion, and he does not have to desire to be made like beauty, for he possesses beauty by love.

St Clement of Alexandria

The Spirit of Love, wherever it is, is its own blessing and happiness, because it is the truth and reality of God in the soul; and therefore is in the same joy of life, and is the same good to itself everywhere and on every occasion. Would you know the blessing of all blessings? It is this God of Love dwelling in your soul, and killing every root of bitterness, which is the pain and torment of every earthly, selfish love. For all wants are satisfied, all disorders of nature are removed, no life is any longer a burden, every day is a day of peace, everything you meet becomes a help to you, because everything you see or do is all done in the sweet, gentle element of Love.

William Law
A Serious Call to the Devout Life

God's Love for Us

Intimate union with his God, into which the Christian can be introduced by Christ, is ultimately a union of love, but a love that could not exist without a certain degree of knowledge of the greatness, the beauty and the truth of God – in short, of all that makes him whom one loves worthy of being loved. How could an unknowable God be loved in truth? How could an impersonal God, in whom I could in no way find the satisfaction of the most imperious needs of my spirit and heart, be held in love? How could a God who would not be both the wellspring of my life and the one who will one day be its eternal fulfilment, captivate me, and how would he have the right to take possession of my life and my love?

René Voillaume
*Contemplation in the
Church of Our Time*

God certainly is well within his rights in claiming to himself the works of his own hands, the gifts he himself has given! How should the thing made fail to love the Maker, provided that it have from him the power to love at all? How should it not love him with all its powers, since only by his gift has it got anything? Man, called into being out of nothing by God's free act and raised to such high honour, how patent is his debt of love to God's most just demand! How vastly God has multiplied his mercy too, in saving man and beast in such a way! Why, we had turned our glory into the likeness of a calf that eateth hay; our sin had brought us to the level of the beasts that know not God at all! If then I owe myself entire to my creator, what shall I give my re-creator more? The means of our remaking took, think what they cost! It was far easier to make than to redeem; for God had but to speak the word and all things were created, I included; but he who made me by a word, and made me once for all, spent on the task of my re-making many words and many marvellous deeds, and suffered grievous and humiliating wrongs.

What reward therefore shall I give the Lord for all the benefits that he has done to me? By his first work he gave me to myself; and by the next he gave himself to me. And when he gave himself, he gave me back myself that I had lost. Myself for myself, given and restored, I doubly owe to him. But what shall I return for himself? A thousand of myself would be as nothing in respect of him.

St Bernard of Clairvaux
On the Love of God

In each soul, God loves and partly saves the whole world which that soul sums up in an incommunicable and particular way.

Pierre Teilhard de Chardin

Love bade me welcome; yet my soul drew back,
   Guilty of dust and sin.
But quick-eyed Love, observing me grow slack
   From my first entrance in,
Drew nearer to me, sweetly questioning
   If I lack'd anything.

'A guest,' I answered, 'worthy to be here.'
   Love said, 'You shall be he.'
'I, the unkind, ungrateful? Ah, my dear,
   I cannot look on Thee.'
Love took my hand and smiling did reply,
   'Who made the eyes but I?'

'Truth, Lord; but I have marr'd them: let my shame
   Go where it doth deserve.'
'And know you not,' says Love, 'who bore the blame?'
   'My dear, then I will serve.'
'You must sit down,' says Love, 'and taste my meat.'
   So I did sit and eat.

George Herbert
'Love', last poem in *The Temple*

That measureless love which is God himself, dwells in the pure deeps of our spirit, like a burning brazier of coals. And it throws forth brilliant and fiery sparks which stir and enkindle heart and senses, will and desire, and all the powers of the soul, with a fire of love.

Jan van Ruysbroeck
The Book of Supreme Truth

No sooner do we believe that God loves us than there is an impulse to believe that he does so, not because he is love, but because we are intrinsically lovable.

C. S. Lewis
The Four Loves

It was at this time that our Lord showed me spiritually how intimately he loves us. I saw that he is everything that we know to be good and helpful. In his love he clothes us, enfolds and embraces us; that tender love completely surrounds us, never to leave us. As I saw it he is everything that is good.

And he showed me more, a little thing, the size of a hazelnut, on the palm of my hand, round like a ball. I looked at it thoughtfully and wondered, 'What is this?' And the answer came, 'It is all that is made.' I marvelled that it continued to exist and did not suddenly disintegrate; it was so small. And again my mind supplied the answer, 'It exists, both now and for ever, because God loves it.' In short, everything owes its existence to the love of God.

In this 'little thing' I saw three truths. The first is that God made it; the second is that God loves it; and the third is that God sustains it. But what he is who is in truth, Maker, Keeper, and Lover I cannot tell, for until I am essentially united with him I can never have full rest or real happiness; in other words, until I am so joined to him that there is absolutely nothing between my God and me. We have got to realize the littleness of creation and to see it for the nothing that it is before we can love and possess God who is uncreated. This is the reason why we have no ease of heart or soul, for we are seeking our rest in trivial things which cannot satisfy, and not seeking to know God, almighty, all-wise, all-good. He is true rest. It is his will that we should know him, and his pleasure that we should rest in him. Nothing less will satisfy us. No soul can rest until it is detached from all creation. When it is deliberately so detached for love of him who is all then only can it experience spiritual rest.

Julian of Norwich
Revelations of Divine Love

Our Love of God

Love is the greatest thing that God can give us; for himself is love: and it is the greatest thing we can give to God; for it will also give ourselves, and carry with it all that is ours. The apostle calls it the band of perfection; it is the old, and it is the new, and it is the great commandment, and it is all the commandments; for it is the fulfilling of the law. It does the work of all other graces without any instrument but its own immediate virtue.

Jeremy Taylor
The Rule of Holy Living

The nearest way to God
Leads through love's open door;
The path of knowledge is
Too slow for evermore.

Angelus Silesius
Selections from *Rhymes of a
German Mystic*

Love demands knowledge, for we can never love the unknown; the more thorough does our knowledge of something good become, the deeper grows our love for it – as long as the emotion meets with no impediment. Still, it often happens that love, due to knowledge, does not keep pace with what the mind perceives, but spurts well on ahead. In this life, then, our love for God can exceed our knowledge of him.

St Francis of Sales
The Love of God

It is but right that our hearts should be on God, when the heart of God is so much on us. If the Lord of glory can stoop so low as to set his heart on sinful dust, methinks we should easily be persuaded to set our hearts on Christ and glory, and ascend to him, in our daily affections, who so much condescends to us. Christian, dost thou not perceive that the heart of God is set upon thee, and that he is still minding thee with tender love, even when thou forgettest both thyself and him? Is he not following thee with daily mercies, moving upon thy soul, providing for thy body, preserving both? Doth he not bear thee continually in the arms of his love, and promise that all things shall work together for thy good, and suit all his dealings to thy greatest advantage, and give his angels charge over thee? And canst thou be taken up with the joys below and forget thy Lord who forgets not thee? Unkind ingratitude! When he speaks of his own kindness for us, hear what he says: 'Zion said, The Lord hath forsaken me, and my Lord hath forgotten me. Can a woman forget her sucking child, that she should not have compassion on the son of her womb? Yea, they may forget, yet will I not forget thee. Behold, I have graven thee upon the palms of my hands; thy walls are continually before me.' But when he speaks of our regards to him, the case is otherwise: 'Can a maid forget her ornaments, or a bride her attire? Yet my people have forgotten me days without number.' As if he should say, 'You will not rise one morning and forget your vanity of dress; and are these of more worth than your God, of more importance than your eternal life? And yet you can forget these day after day.' Let us not give God cause thus to expostulate with us. Rather let our souls get up to God, and visit him every morning, and our hearts be towards him every moment.

Richard Baxter
The Saints' Everlasting Rest

If we truly love ourselves, and all other creatures that are to be loved, only in God and for God, what else do we love in ourselves and in them but him? For when God is loved by us with our whole heart and our whole mind, then without doubt our neighbour and everything that we love is most properly loved. If therefore we pour forth our heart before God and in the love of God, being bound to him and held fast to him, what more is there with which we may love any other thing whatever? Verily, in the love of God is the love of one's neighbour. Therefore, as he that loves God cannot but love man, so he that truly loves Christ is proved to love nothing in him but God. Also we yield all that we are loved by or that we love to God, the Well of Love; for he commands all man's heart to be given to himself, and wishes all dispositions and workings of the mind to be fixed in him. Moreover, he that truly loves God perceives nothing else, he has nothing else. But whatsoever he has, he loves for God, and he loves nothing but what God wishes him to love. Wherefore, he loves nothing but God, and so God is all his love.

Richard Rolle
The Fire of Love

'It is fire that I have come to spread over the earth, and what better can I wish than it should be kindled' (Luke 12:49). It is the Master himself who here reveals his desire to see kindled the fire of love. Actually, all our works, and labours, are as nothing in his sight. We can give him nothing nor can we satisfy his one desire which is to restore the dignity of our soul. Nothing pleases him so much as to see that dignity increase, and nothing can so exalt it as our becoming in a sense God's equal. That is why he demands of us the tribute of our love, the property of love being to make lover and beloved, as far as possible, equal. The soul in possession of this love appears on a footing of equality with Jesus Christ, because their reciprocal affection makes all things common between them. 'I have made known to you all that my Father has told me, and so I have called you my friends' (John 14:15). But in order to arrive at this love, the soul must first have surrendered herself entirely; her will must be sweetly lost in that of God, so that her inclinations and her faculties move henceforth only in this love and for this love. I do everything with love, I endure everything with love, this is what David meant when he sang: 'My citadel is God himself, the God who loves me' (Psalm 59:10). Then love so fills, absorbs and protects her that she finds everywhere the secret of growing in love; even in the midst of her dealings with the world, in the midst of life's troubles, she has the right to say: 'My sole occupation is to love.'

Blessed Elizabeth of the Trinity
Selected Writings

Everyone that loves is made like to his Beloved and love makes him who loves like unto that which is loved.

Richard Rolle
The Fire of Love

'I love and love not; Lord, it breaks my heart
    To love and not to love.
Thou veiled within Thy glory, gone apart
    Into Thy shrine which is above,
Dost Thou not love me, Lord, or care
    For this mine ill?'

'I love thee here or there,
    I will accept thy broken heart – lie still.'

'Lord, it was well with me in time gone by
    That cometh not again,
When I was fresh and cheerful, who but I?
    I fresh, I cheerful: worn with pain
Now out of sight and out of heart;
    O Lord, how long?'

'I watch thee as thou art,
    I will accept thy fainting heart – be strong.'

'Lie still, be strong, today: but, Lord, tomorrow,
    What of tomorrow, Lord?
Shall there be rest from toil, be truce from
    sorrow,
    Be living gree upon the sward,

Now but a barren grave to me,
Be joy for sorrow?'

'Did I not die for thee?
Do I not live for thee? Leave me tomorrow.'

Christina Rossetti

Love of Neighbour

Our Lord asks but two things of us: Love for him, and for our neighbour: this is what we must strive to obtain . . . We cannot know whether we love God, although there may be strong reasons for thinking so, but there can be no doubt about whether we love our neighbour or no. Be sure that in proportion as you advance in fraternal charity you are increasing in your love of God. In this most important matter we should be most watchful in little things, and take no notice of the great works we plan during prayer . . . It is amusing to see souls who, while they are at prayer, fancy they are willing to be despised and publicly insulted for the love of God, yet afterwards do all they can to hide their small defects; if anyone unjustly accuses them of a fault, God deliver us from their outcries! Let those who cannot bear such things take no notice of the splendid plan they made when alone . . .

Prayer does not consist of such fancies . . . No, our Lord expects *works* from us . . . Beg our Lord to grant you perfect love for your neighbour . . . If someone else is well spoken of, be more pleased than if it were yourself; this is easy enough, for if you were really humble, it would vex you to be praised.

. . . Force your will, as far as possible, to comply in all things with [others'] wishes although sometimes you may lose your own rights by doing so. Forget your self-interests for theirs, however much nature may rebel.

St Teresa of Avila
The Interior Castle

I thought Love lived in the hot sunshine,
But O he lives in the moony light!
I thought to find Love in the heat of day,
But sweet Love is the comforter of night.

Seek Love in the pity of others' woe,
In the gentle relief of another's care,
In the darkness of night and the winter's snow,
In the naked and outcast, seek Love there.

William Blake
William Bond

Be fixed and unshaken in your faith; care for each other with a brother's love, and make common cause for the truth. Give way to one another in the Lord's own spirit of courtesy, treating no one as inferior. When it is in your power to do a kindness, never put it off to another time, for charity is death's reprieve.

St Polycarp
Letter to the Philippians

I saw myself, a youth, almost a boy, in a low pitched wooden church. The slim wax candles gleamed, spots of red, before the old pictures of the Saints. There stood before me many people, all fair-haired peasant heads. From time to time, they began swaying, falling, rising again, like the ripe ears of wheat when the wind in summer passes over them. All at once a man came up from behind and stood beside me. I did not turn towards him, but I felt that the man was Christ. Emotion, curiosity, awe overmastered me. I made an effort and looked at my neighbour. A face like everyone's, a face like all men's faces. The eyes looked a little upward; quietly and intently; the lips closed, not compressed; the upper lip as it were resting on the other; a small beard parted in two; the hands folded and still; and the clothes on him, like everyone's. 'What sort of Christ is this?' I thought. 'Such an ordinary, ordinary man. It cannot be.' I turned away, but I had hardly turned my eyes from this ordinary man when I felt again that it was really none other than Christ standing beside me. Suddenly my heart sank and I came to myself. Only then I realized that just such a face is the face of Christ – a face like all men's faces.

Ivan Turgenev
Novels and Stories

O Christ, in this man's life
This stranger who is Thine – in all his strife,
All his felicity, his good and ill
In the assaulted stronghold of his will;

I do confess Thee here,
Alive within this life; I know Thee near
Within this lonely conscience, closed away
Within this brother's solitary day.

Christ in his unknown heart,
His intellect unknown, this love, this art,
This battle and this peace, this destiny
That I shall never know, look upon me.

Christ in his numbered breath,
Christ in his beating heart and in his death,
Christ in his mystery! From that secret place,
And from that separate dwelling, give me grace!

Alice Meynell
The Unknown Christ

Though we do not have our Lord with us in bodily presence, we have our neighbour, who, for the ends of love and loving service, is as good as our Lord himself.

St Teresa of Avila

Certainly whatever we do to the least of our brothers, we do to God, and no one could love God if he did not love his brother. It is, therefore, a matter of one and the same direction of love, but bearing on two objects, for God remains distinct from our brothers and deserves to be loved for himself. Christ lives in the hearts of men, but what I can reach in my brothers is not God in person, nor is it Christ himself, but his image, his presence through grace, the marvels of his love and mercy, which are in their own way admirable objects of contemplation. But if we content ourselves with seeking God by loving our brothers and giving ourselves to them generously, would it not be still to remain somehow closed up within the limits themselves of humanity? Would we then be capable uniquely of contemplating man, in his mystery to be sure, but also in his limits? Would we be reduced to contemplating the works of the Lord without being able to contemplate the Lord himself? I hardly dare add that a Christian who would be no longer concerned to contemplate the Lord Jesus and love him above all else would no longer be capable, whatever the generosity of his gift to the service of men, of loving them as Jesus loves them. Only in the contemplation of the Heart of Christ can we rejoin in its fullness the source of this love of friendship of divine quality which is poured out to men and which every Christian should strive constantly to share.

René Voillaume
Contemplation in the Church
of Our Time

Next to the Blessed Sacrament itself, your neighbour is the holiest object presented to your senses. If he is your Christian neighbour, he is holy in almost the same way, for in him also Christ *vere latitat* – the glorifier and the glorified, Glory Himself, is truly hidden.

C. S. Lewis

There is a grace of kind listening, as well as a grace of kind speaking. Some men listen with an abstracted air, which shows that their thoughts are elsewhere. Or they seem to listen, but by wide answers and irrelevant questions show that they have been occupied with their own thoughts, as being more interesting, at least in their own estimation, than what you have been saying. Some listen with a kind of importunate ferocity which makes you feel that you are being put upon your trial, and that your auditor expects beforehand that you are going to tell him a lie, or to be inaccurate, or to say something which he will disapprove, and that you must mind your expressions. Some interrupt, and will not hear you to the end. Some hear you to the end, and then forthwith begin to talk to you about a similar experience which has befallen themselves, making your case only an illustration of their own. Some, meaning to be kind, listen with such a determined, lively, violent attention that you are at once made uncomfortable, and the charm of conversation is at an end. Many persons whose manners will stand the test of speaking, break down under the trial of listening. But all these things should be brought under the sweet influence of religion. Kind listening is often an act of the most delicate interior mortification, and is a great assistance towards kind speaking.

Frederick William Faber
Spiritual Conferences

Be kind, be kind, and you will be Saints.

Jan van Ruysbroeck

Chapter Four

Misplaced Love

Love of Self

The love of our neighbour is the only door out of the dungeon of self.

George MacDonald

Self-love, being the enemy of the love of God, is consequently the enemy of that lawful and well-ordered love which we should have for ourselves. Reason and faith equally concur in making it a duty for me to love my true, sovereign and sole good; and both teach me that this supreme good is and can only be God. Faith goes further and tells me that if I love God in this life in the manner he has ordained, I shall see and possess him eternally, with a love which will constitute my supreme happiness. Now self-love, by setting my affections on my *self* (which is not and can never be my chief good and the source of my happiness) draws me away from loving my sovereign and unique good. It exposes me to the danger of being for ever deprived of the joy of possessing God, and it is certain that I shall never enter into that complete possession of him so long as there remains the least vestige of self-love within me. I have, therefore, no greater interest, apart from being preserved from mortal sin, than to be entirely freed from self-love, since upon this my whole happiness depends.

John Nicholas Grou
Meditations on the Love of God

That love, which we call hope, is a self-regarding love, but it is a saintly, well-regulated love of self. We are not drawing God down to our own level, turning him to our advantage; we are uniting ourselves to him as our last end, our final happiness. We love ourselves as well as God, but we do not put ourselves on the same level as him, or even prefer ourselves to him. Self-love is all mixed up with our love for God, but love of him floats to the top. Self-love clearly enters into our love for God, but as a mere motive, not the chief end in view. We are to some extent thinking of ourselves, but God holds first place. Yes, there is no doubt of it: when we love God as our supreme good, we are not loving him for a quality which brings him down to us, but for one which lifts us up, brings us home to him. We are not his goal, his ambition, his perfection; but he is ours. He is not our property, we are his; he does not depend on us, we depend on him. In a word: as our supreme good, which we love, he gains nothing from us, but we gain all from him. He is rich and beautiful in our regard; we are merely expressing our wants, our poverty. Loving God as our supreme good, then, is in no way dishonourable or disrespectful; we are acknowledging him to be our perfection, our refreshment, our goal, in the possession of which our happiness lies.

St Francis of Sales
The Love of God

He who hates not in himself his self-love and that instinct which leads him to make himself a God, is indeed blind.

Blaise Pascal
Pensées

Every intelligent being capable of happiness must necessarily love himself. If he finds his perfection and happiness within him, his love is called one of complacence. He cannot covet anything, because he already has all he could wish for, and nothing else has any attraction for him. Such is the love God has for himself, and he is the only being who can love himself thus. All other beings have been drawn out of nothingness and owing to God whatever they possess, cannot find their happiness within themselves and cannot therefore love themselves with a love of complacence, and can only truly and legitimately love themselves by loving the one from whom they have received everything and from whom they expect their ultimate happiness, and who is consequently their sovereign Good. For 'whoever does not love God,' says St Augustine, 'does not love himself.' This is the true love for myself that not only I may but must have: I must love God who alone is supremely worthy of love in himself and the source of any good that is in me, and the possession of whom alone can make me happy. No created being has the right to love himself in any other way, and this love of myself, properly understood and controlled, has nothing in common with self-love as we know it, since it is God's own love reflected in us.

John Nicholas Grou
Meditations on the Love of God

People who love themselves aright, even as they ought to love their neighbour, bear charitably, though without flattery, with self as with another. They know what needs correction at home as well as elsewhere; they strive heartily and vigorously to correct it, but they deal with self as they would deal with someone else they wished to bring to God. They set to work patiently, not exacting more than is practicable under present circumstances from themselves any more than from others, and not being disheartened because perfection is not attainable in a day.

François Fenelon
Letters to Women

We may desire to be stripped of our self-love by another self-love. We can desire and love humility through pride. Without question there is in our actions and interior dispositions a perpetual circle and incessant return of ourselves upon ourselves, which is almost imperceptible. There always remains in our heart a root of self-love which is extremely fine, subtle, and volatile, and which is unknown to us. So that we are sometimes very far from guiding ourselves by reasons altogether divine and motives purely disinterested, at the very moment when we think we are doing so the most completely. Job's comforters are examples of this. Pure and true love of God, disengaged from all consideration of self, is extremely rare and exceedingly difficult.

Frederick William Faber
Growth in Holiness

In your excessive self-love you are like a molecule closed in upon itself and incapable of entering easily into any new combination. God looks to you to be more open and more pliant. If you are to enter into him you need to be freer and more eager. Have done, then, with your egoism and your fear of suffering.

Pierre Teilhard de Chardin
Let Me Explain

A soul that desires to attain knowledge of spiritual things must first know itself, for it cannot acquire knowledge of a higher kind until it first knows itself. The soul does this when it is so recollected and detached from all earthly preoccupations and from the influence of the senses that it understands itself as it is in its own nature, taking no account of the body. So if you desire to know and see your soul as it is, do not look for it within your body as though it were hidden in your heart in the same way that the heart is hidden within the body. If you look for it in this way you will never find it. The more you search for it as for a material object, the further you are from it, for your soul is not tangible, but a living and invisible spirit. It is not hidden and enclosed in your body in the way that a lesser object is hidden and enclosed within a greater; on the contrary, it is the soul that sustains and gives life to the body, and is possessed of much greater strength and virtue.

Therefore, if you desire to discover your soul, withdraw your thoughts from outward and material things, forgetting if possible your own body and its five senses, and consider the nature of a rational soul in the same way as you would consider any virtue, such as truth or humility. Similarly, consider how the soul is a living spirit, immortal and invisible, with power in itself to see and know supreme truth and to love supreme good, which is God. Once you have grasped this, you have some understanding of yourself. Do not seek this knowledge in any other way, for the more clearly and fully you can study the nature and dignity of a rational soul – what it is, and how it functions – the better you will understand yourself.

Walter Hilton
The Scale of Perfection

There is hardly a man or woman in the world who has not got some corner of self into which he or she fears to venture with a light. The reasons for this may be various, as various as the individual souls. Nevertheless, in spite of the variety of reasons, the fact is universal. For the most part we hardly know our own reasons. It is an instinct, one of the quick instincts of corrupt nature. We prophesy to ourselves that, if we penetrate into that corner of self, something will have to be done which either our laziness or our immortification would shrink from doing. If we enter that sanctuary, some charm of easy devotion or smooth living will be broken. We shall find ourselves face to face with something unpleasant, something which will perhaps constrain us to all the trouble and annoyance of a complete interior revolution, or else leave us very uncomfortable in conscience. We may perhaps be committed to something higher than our present way of life, and that is out of the question. Religion is yoke enough as it is. So we leave this corner of self curtained off, locked up like a room in a house with disagreeable associations attached to it, unvisited like a lumber closet where we are conscious that disorder and dirt are accumulating, which we have not just now the vigour to grapple with. But do we think that God cannot enter there except by our unlocking the door? Or see anything when he is there, unless we hold him a light? . . .

We know how his eye rests upon us incessantly, and takes us all in, and searches us out, and as it were burns us up with his holy gaze. His perfections environ us with the most awful nearness, flooding us with insupportable light. To his eye there is not only no concealment, there is not even a softening shade, or a distance to subdue the harshness and veil the unworthiness. Yet, for all this, to be straight-forward with God is neither an easy nor a common grace.

O with what unutterable faith must we believe in our own falsehood, when we can feel it to be anything like a shelter in the presence of the all-seeing God!

Frederick William Faber
Spiritual Conferences (1859)

Humility

My mind is made to see God, and I am always looking at myself. Humility comes to correct my vision. And the first thing that humility tells me is that I have nothing of myself. It does not say that I have nothing at all, but that I have nothing through myself. I do not exist of myself, and nothing that I have comes of myself. Neither my existence, nor any of the gifts of existence in me, is through myself. What I have of myself is nothing.

Through myself I get sin, the tendency to evil, weakness, imperfection and all the miseries the witness of which I bear in myself.

And humility, which is truth, makes me see and recognize the nothingness which I am of myself. It does not frown at the lessons of its own nothingness, which are given to man in so many of his experiences and in so many shapes. To acknowledge one's sins and mistakes, not to persist in one's own views, to admit one's imperfections and shortcomings, to accept inward and outward humiliations, to draw conclusions preferably against oneself and in favour of others, etc., this is what is suggested by humility.

True humility neither misjudges, nor denies, nor lessens any of God's gifts. It too well understands the responsibility

74

for talents received. It recognizes natural gifts and super-natural gifts, and knows whence they come. And when these gifts, which are recognized by it and used owing to it, yield their fruits, it knows that these fruits are to be attributed to the Giver of the gifts that yield them. It sees so clearly that it has nothing which it has not received, and it takes good care not to glory in them as if it had not received them (1 Corinthians 4:7).

Joseph Tissot
The Interior Life

He who is truly humble is never astonished at his falls. He knows that man is so feeble he can do nothing without the assistance of God.

Frederick William Faber
Growth in Holiness

Peace of soul and patience are inseparably bound up with humility. However, I do not call obsequious words and gestures, or bowings and scrapings, humility; especially when they are done, as frequently happens, with no inner conviction of self-abasement, no due regard for one's neighbour. All it amounts to is the play-acting of weak minds – humility's shadow, not its substance. The humility I mean is dignified, genuine, deep-rooted and solid; a quality that makes us docile to correction, tractable and prompt to obey.

St Francis of Sales
The Love of God

The reason why God is so great a Lover of humility is because he is the great Lover of truth. Now humility is nothing but truth, while pride is nothing but lying.

St Vincent de Paul

Humility, that is lowliness or self-abasement, is an inward bowing down or prostrating of the heart and of the conscience before God's transcendent worth. Righteousness demands and orders this, and through charity a loving heart cannot leave it undone. When a lowly and loving man considers that God has served him so humbly, so lovingly, and so faithfully; and sees God so high, so mighty, and so noble, and man so poor, and so little, and so low; then there springs up within the humble heart a great awe and a great veneration for God. For to pay homage to God by every outward and inward act, this is the first and dearest work of humility, the most savoury among those of charity, and the most meet among those of righteousness. The loving and humble heart cannot pay homage enough either to God or to his noble manhood, nor can it abase itself as much as it would. And that is why a humble man thinks that his worship of God and his lowly service are always falling short. And he is meek, reverencing Holy Church and the sacraments. And he is discreet in food and drink, in speech, in the answers which he makes to everybody; and in his behaviour, dress, and lowly service he is without hyprocrisy and without pretence. And he is humble in his devotions, both outwardly and inwardly, before God and before all men, so that none is offended because of him. And so he overcomes and casts out pride, which is the source and origin of all other sins. By humility the snares of the devil, and of sin, and of the world are broken, and man is set in order and established in the very condition of virtue. And heaven is open to him, and God stoops to hear his prayers, and he is fulfilled with grace. And Christ, that strong rock, is his foundation. Whosoever therefore grounds his virtue in humility, he shall never err.

Jan van Ruysbroeck
The Adornment of the
Spiritual Marriage

Sin

The Christian, in fact, possesses two lives – the life of Adam and that of our Lord; the life of the flesh and that of the Spirit. These two lives are opposed to each other; it is needful for one to be wholly annihilated in order that the other become absolutely perfect. Now, so long as we are here below, the life of the flesh is never wholly destroyed. By a special privilege, however, and in reward for heroic mortifications or for great faithfulness to the Holy Spirit, it happens to the soul to feel itself occasionally dead to this imperfect life; but this is never other than for a time and in part. Moreover, the life of Jesus Christ within us is never in this world so peaceful or wholly perfect. We must always have the sword in hand in order to overcome our enemies and those of God; it is always necessary for us to labour in order to mortify and destroy the old man.

Jean-Jacques Olier
Pensées choisies

We are created to will what God wills, to know what he knows, to love what he loves. Sin is the will to do what God does not will, to know what he does not know, to love what he does not love.

Thomas Merton
No Man is an Island

O child, hast though fallen? Arise, and go, with childlike trust, to thy father, like the prodigal son, and humbly say, with heart and mouth, 'Father, I have sinned against heaven, and before thee, and am no more worthy to be called thy son; make me as one of thy hired servants.' And what will thy heavenly father do but what that father did in the parable? Assuredly he will not change his essence, which is love, for the sake of thy misdoings. Is it not his own precious treasure, and a small thing with him to forgive thee thy trespasses, if thou believe in him? For his hand is not shortened that it cannot make thee fit to be saved.

John Tauler
Sermons on the Inner Way

Our faults are like a grain of sand beside the great mountain of the mercies of God.

St Jean-Baptiste Vianney
Sermons

Discouragement is no part of genuine penance. It atones for nothing, satisfies for nothing, merits nothing, impetrates nothing. It does not make us more careful next time: rather the opposite, for, by dejecting us it makes us at once more open to temptation and less masculine in resisting it. But on the contrary there is much good in not being cast down. We shall be less teased with the imperfection in ourselves, and more occupied with the infidelity to God. To fall and not to be out of spirits with the fall is not only to keep the courage we had, but to gain more. It is the humblest course, and on that account the most acceptable to God. It is the most reasonable, and therefore has the greater blessing.

Frederick William Faber
Growth in Holiness

Nothing should grieve us, not even our faults. For all the more reason, then, we ought not to allow ourselves to be despondent over the lamentable results of certain actions which are not sins, however much they may indicate imprudence on our part. Few ordeals are more mortifying to self-love; and, it follows, few are more sanctifying. It does not cost us nearly as much to accept humiliations which come from without and which we have in no way drawn upon ourselves. We are much more readily resigned to the shame caused by faults far graver in themselves, provided that there is no outward evidence of them. But a mere imprudence which has lamentable consequences that are plain for all to see is obviously the most humiliating of all humiliations, and provides, therefore, an excellent opportunity for destroying self-love. Never fail to take advantage of it. For then we have our hearts entirely in our power; we can compel them, despite their resistance, to make an act of complete resignation. It is at such times that we must repeat not once, but many times, the *fiat* of a perfect resignation; you must endeavour even to render thanks, adding a *Gloria Patri* to the *fiat*.

Jean-Pierre de Caussade
Self-Abandonment to Divine Providence (Letters)

Temptation

We are like coral. In the sea, where it grows, it is a pale green, fragile and flexible shrub; taken from the sea bed, it becomes rigid, stone-like, while its colour changes to a bright red. We are prone, from our birth in the ocean of this world, to go from one extreme to the other, bending this way and that — now drawn towards love of God by inspiration, now drawn to love of earthly things by temptation. Taken out of this life, the pale green of trembling hope transformed into the bright red of assured fruition, we shall sway from side to side no longer, arrested for ever in eternal love.

It is impossible to see God and not love him. Here below, where we catch only a glimpse of him through the clouds of faith, like *a confused reflection in a mirror* (1 Corinthians 13:12), we do not come to know him well enough to prevent other apparently good things from finding their way through the mists which surround the certainty and truth of faith. Like little foxes, they steal in unperceived, *thieving among our vineyards all a-blossoming* (Cant. 2:15).

What it comes to is this: once charity is ours, free will wears the wedding garment. We can keep it on by doing good, or take it off by sinning, just as we please.

St Francis of Sales
The Love of God

No man is so perfect and holy as not to have sometimes temptations; and we cannot be wholly without them.

Thomas à Kempis
The Imitation of Christ

Abbot Pastor said that Abbot John the Dwarf had prayed to the Lord and the Lord had taken away all his passions, so that he became impassible. And in this condition he went to one of the elders and said: You see before you a man who is completely at rest and has no more temptations. The elder said: Go and pray to the Lord to command some struggle to be stirred up in you, for the soul is matured only in battles. And when the temptations started up again he did not pray that the struggle be taken away from him, but only said: Lord, give me strength to get through the fight.

The Sayings of the Desert Fathers

There are but two things that we can do against temptations. The first is to be faithful to the light within us, in avoiding all exposure to temptation which we are at liberty to avoid. I say, all that we are at liberty to avoid, because it does not always depend upon ourselves whether we shall escape occasions of sin. Those that belong to the situation in life in which Providence has placed us are not under our control. The other is to turn our eyes to God in the moment of temptation, to throw ourselves immediately upon the protection of heaven, as a child when in danger flies to the arms of its parents.

The habitual conviction of the presence of God is the sovereign remedy; it supports, it consoles, it calms us. We must not be surprised that we are tempted. We are placed here to be proved by temptations. Everything is temptation to us. Crosses irritate our pride and prosperity flatters it; our life is a continual warfare, but Jesus Christ combats with us. We must let temptations, like a tempest, beat upon our heads, and still move on; like a traveller surprised on the way by a storm, who wraps his cloak about him, and goes on his journey in spite of the opposing elements.

In a certain sense, there is little to do in doing the will of God. Still it is true that it is a great work, because it must be without any reserve. His Spirit enters the secret folding of our hearts, and even the most upright affections and the most necessary attachments must be regulated by his will; but it is not the multitude of hard duties, it is not the constraint and contention, that advances us on our course. On the contrary it is the yielding of our wills without restriction to tread cheerfully every day in the path in which Providence leads us; to seek nothing, to be discouraged by nothing, to see our duty in the present moment, to trust all else without reserve to the will and power of God.

François Fenelon
Letters and Reflections

What are the uses of temptation?

Temptations try us and we are worth nothing if we are not tried.

Temptations disgust us with the world almost effectually as the sweetness which God gives us in prayer.

Temptations enable us to merit more, they increase our love of God.

Temptations purify us for God's presence.

Temptations teach us our own weakness and so humble us.

Temptations give us a greater esteem of grace; grace grows by being esteemed.

Temptations make virtue take deeper root, and so play their part in the grand grace of final perseverance.

Temptations make us more watchful and so instead of leading into sin, they hinder shoals of sins.

Temptations teach us self-knowledge.

Frederick William Faber
Growth in Holiness

The craftsman beats gold with his hammer to get rid of the dross. He assiduously scrapes away with his file so that the vein of glittering metal may gleam more brightly. 'Just as the potter's jar is tried in the furnace so are just men tried by temptation.' That is why St James says, 'Count it all joy, my brethren, when you meet various trials.'

Peter Damian
A Letter

Treat such small temptations like flies and gnats which flutter about us and sometimes settle on the face; as we cannot be entirely rid of them our best defence is to remain undisturbed; they can annoy us but never harm us so long as we are firmly resolved to serve God. Despise such temptations without listening to them; treat them like flies; let them hover all around you and buzz about your ears as much as they like; when they settle on your heart and try to sting you, do not attack them or argue with them but merely drive them away quietly by making acts of love of God or of any other virtue; or if you have had time to recognize the real nature of the temptation, by an act of the contrary virtue; then turn your heart to Christ Crucified and in spirit kiss his feet by an act of love, for to persist in acts of the contrary virtue would be to dispute with the temptation.

An act of the love of God is the surest weapon against temptations great and small; for the love of God contains to an eminent degree the perfection of all the virtues and is the most perfect remedy for vice. Learn to seek peace in this remedy whenever temptations trouble you, and you will have no need to examine or consider them; moreover the devil will be so terrified when he sees that these temptations lead you to make acts of the love of God that he will cease to trouble you. So much for these countless small temptations, to give more attention to them would only be a waste of time.

St Francis of Sales
Introduction to the
Devout Life

Chapter Five

Dying, We Live

Dying, We Live

The golden apple of selfhood, thrown among the false gods, became an apple of discord because they scrambled for it. They did not know the first rule of the holy game, which is that every player must by all means touch the ball and then immediately pass it on. To be found with it in your hands is a fault: to cling to it, death. But when it flies to and fro among the players too swift for eye to follow, and the great Master himself leads the revelry, giving himself eternally to his creatures in the generation, and back to himself in the sacrifice, of the Word, then indeed the eternal dance 'makes heaven drowsy with the harmony'. All pains and pleasures we have known on earth are early initiations in the movements of that dance: but the dance itself is strictly incomparable with the sufferings of this present time. As we draw nearer to its uncreated rhythm, pain and pleasure sink almost out of sight. There is joy in the dance, but it does not exist for the sake of joy. It does not even exist for the sake of good, or of love. It is Love himself, and Good himself, and therefore happy. It does not exist for us, but we for it . . . As our earth is to all the stars, so doubtless are we men and our concerns to all creation; as all the stars are to space itself, so are all creatures, all thrones and powers and mightiest of the created gods, to the abyss of the self-existing Being, who is to us Father and Redeemer and indwelling Comforter, but of whom no man nor angel can say nor conceive what he is in and for himself, or what is the work that he 'maketh from the beginning to the end'. For they are all derived and unsubstantial things. Their vision fails them and they cover their eyes from the intolerable light of utter actuality, which was and is and shall be, which never could have been otherwise, which has no opposite.

C. S. Lewis
The Problem of Pain

The more thou thine own self
Out of thyself dost throw
The more will into thee
God with his Godhead flow.

Angelus Silesius
Selection from
Rhymes of a German Mystic

It daily becomes more apparent that God's respect for the freedom of our affections, thoughts, and purposes is complete. It is part of that respect for our freedom that he never forces upon us his own gifts. He offers them, but unless we actively accept them, they remain ineffective as far as we are concerned. 'Behold, I stand at the door and knock' – that is always the relation of God our Redeemer to our souls. He has paid the whole price; he has suffered the atoning death; yet still he waits till we open the door of our hearts to let in his love which will call our love out. He never breaks down that door. He stands and knocks. And this is true not only of his first demand for admission to the mansion of the soul; it is true also of every room within that mansion. There are many of us who have opened the front door to him, but only let him into the corridors and staircases; all the rooms where we work or amuse ourselves are still closed against him. There are still greater multitudes who have welcomed him to some rooms, and hope that he will not ask what goes on behind the doors of others. But sooner or later he asks; and if we do not at once take him to see, he leaves the room where we were so comfortable with him, and stands knocking at the closed door. And then we can never again have the joy of his presence in the first room until we open the door at which he is now knocking. We can only have him with us in the room that we choose for him, if we really make him free of all the house.

William Temple
Personal Religion and the
Life of Fellowship

If Christ were to come at this moment, would he find faith on the earth – in us? Where is our faith? What are the proofs of it? Do we believe that this life is only a short passage to a better? Do we believe that we must suffer with Jesus before we can reign with him? Do we look upon the world as a vain show, and death as the entrance into true happiness? Do we live by faith? Does it animate us? Do we enjoy the eternal truths that it presents to us? Do we feed our souls with them, as we nourish our bodies with healthful aliment? Do we accustom ourselves to view everything with the eye of faith? Alas! instead of living by faith, we extinguish it in our souls. How can we truly believe what we profess to believe, and act as we act?

May we not fear, lest the kingdom of heaven be taken from us, and given to others who will bring forth more fruit? This kingdom of heaven is faith, when it swells and reigns in the heart. Blessed are the eyes that see this kingdom; flesh and blood have not seen it; earthly wisdom is blind to it. To realize its glories, we must be born again, and to do this we must die to self.

François Fenelon
Selections from Fenelon

The disciple said to his master: 'How may I come to the supersensual life so that I can see God and hear him speak?' The master said: 'When you can leap for a moment into that where no creature dwells then you can hear what God speaks.'

DISCIPLE: 'Is it near or far?' MASTER: 'It is within you. Could you halt volition and thought for but one hour then you could hear God's inexpressible words.'

DISCIPLE: 'How can I hear when I stop volition and thought?' MASTER: 'When you stop willing and thinking self then the eternal hearing, seeing and speaking will be revealed within you, and God will see and hear through you. Your ego-centric hearing, willing and seeing hinders you from seeing and hearing God.'

DISCIPLE: 'With what shall I see and hear God, since he is beyond nature and creature?' MASTER: 'When you are silent then you are as God was before nature and creature came to be, just like the essence out of which he created your natural, creaturely existence. Then you will hear and see by the same means with which God "saw" and "heard" within you before your ego-centric willing, seeing, and hearing began.'

DISCIPLE: 'But what prevents me from achieving this?' MASTER: 'Your ego-centric willing, hearing and seeing hinders you. You are also hindered by your striving against that out of which you came. By your ego-centric will you break yourself off from God's will, and with your ego-centric

seeing you see only into your own will. And by the self-centredness of earthly, material things your ego-centric will plugs up your hearing, leading you into a "ground", and overshadowing you with that which you do will so that you cannot come to the supernatural, supersensual life.'
DISCIPLE: 'Standing as I do within nature, how may I come through nature into the ground of supersensuality without destroying nature?' MASTER: 'For that three things are necessary: the first is that you must give your ego-centric will over to God. The second is that you must hate your ego-centric will so that you do not do that to which your own will drives you. The third is that you prostrate yourself patiently before the Cross of Our Lord Jesus Christ in order to bear the temptations of nature and creature yourself. And when you do this God will speak into you. He will bring your resigned will into himself, into the supernatural ground, and then you will hear what the Lord speaks within you.'

Jacob Boehme
The Way to Christ

One secret act of self-denial, one sacrifice of inclination to duty, is worth all the mere good thoughts, warm feelings, passionate prayers, in which idle people indulge themselves.

John Henry Newman

Go on, then, ordering your lives in Christ Jesus our Lord . . . You are to be rooted in him, built up in him, your faith established in the teaching you have received, overflowing with gratitude (Colossians 2:6–7).
Go on ordering your lives in Christ Jesus. I think this means to forsake self, forget about self, renounce self in order

to enter more deeply into him with every passing minute; so to enter into him as to be *rooted* in him, and be able to challenge everything that happens with this proud boast: Who will separate us from the love of Christ? When the soul is thus deeply established in him, thus deeply *rooted* in him, the divine sap floods into her, and all that is imperfect, commonplace and natural in her life is destroyed. Then says the Apostle: 'Our mortal nature is swallowed up in life' (2 Corinthians 5:4). The soul thus stripped of self and clothed in Christ need no longer fear external contacts, nor interior difficulties, for, far from being an obstacle, they only root her more securely in love for her Master. No matter what happens, come what may, she continues to adore him, for his own sake, because she is free, liberated from self and detached from everything. She can sing with the Psalmist: 'Though a whole host were arrayed against me, my heart would be undaunted; though an armed onset should threaten me, still would I not lose my confidence . . . for the Lord hides me in the inmost recess of his royal tent' (Psalm 27:3,5), and this royal tent is no other than himself. That, I think is what St Paul means when he speaks of being 'rooted in Jesus Christ'.

Blessed Elizabeth of the Trinity
Spiritual Writings

To deny one's self is to be the only begotten Son of God and one who does so has for himself all the properties of that Son. All God's acts are performed and his teachings conveyed through the Son, to the point that we should be his only begotten Son. And when this is accomplished in God's sight, he is so fond of us and so fervent that he acts as if his divine Being might be shattered and he himself annihilated if the whole foundations of his Godhead were not revealed to us, together with his nature and being. God makes haste to do this, so that it may be ours as it is his. It is here that God finds joy and rapture in fulfilment and the person who is thus within God's knowing and love becomes just what God himself is.

If you love yourself, you love everybody else as you do yourself. As long as you love another person less than you love yourself, you will not really succeed in loving yourself but if you love all alike, including yourself, you will love them as one person and that person is both God and man. Thus he is a just and righteous person who, loving himself, loves all others equally.

Meister Eckhart
Sermons

The Indwelling

That God is present in all places, that he sees every action, hears all discourses, and understands every thought, is no strange thing to a Christian ear, who hath been taught his doctrine not only by right reason and the consent of all the wise men in the world, but also by God himself in Holy Scripture. 'I am a God at hand, saith the Lord, and not a God far off.' Can any hide himself in secret places, that I shall not see him? said the Lord; do not I fill heaven and earth? 'Neither is there any creature that is not manifest in his sight; but all things are naked and open before the eyes of him with whom we have to do.' 'In him we live and move and have our being.' God is wholly in every place, included in no place; not bound with bands except those of love; not divided into parts, not changeable into several shapes; filling heaven and earth with his present power and with his never absent nature. So that we may imagine God and be as the air and the sea, and we are all enclosed in this circle, wrapped up in the lap of this infinite nature, or as infants in the wombs of their pregnant mothers; and we can no more be removed from the presence of God than from our own being . . .

God is especially present in the hearts of his people, by his Holy Spirit, and indeed the hearts of holy men are temples in the truth of things, and in type and shadow they are heaven itself. For God reigns in the hearts of his servants; there is his kingdom. The power of grace hath subdued all his enemies; there is his power. They serve him night and day, and give him thanks and praise; that is his glory. This is the religion and worship of God in the temple. The temple itself is the heart of man, Christ is the high priest, who from thence sends up the incense of prayers, and joins them to his own intercession and presents all together to his Father; and the Holy Ghost by his dwelling there hath also consecrated it into a temple, and God dwells in our hearts by faith, and Christ by his Spirit, and the Spirit by his purities; so that we are also cabinets of the mysterious Trinity, and what is this short of heaven itself, but as infancy is short of manhood and letters of words? The same state of life it is, but yet true, representing the beauties of the soul, and the grace of God, and the images of his eternal glory, by the reality of a special presence.

Jeremy Taylor
The Rule of Holy Living

God is present in my heart, since the desire for the pursuit of happiness never leaves it. This desire is its very life and is essential to it. But to desire a thing is to long to be united to it, to enjoy the possession of it. If, therefore, God is the only real and essential happiness, as we cannot doubt, it follows obviously that my heart must desire him continually, naturally and necessarily, from a deep instinct and an intimate principle by which it knows and pursues what is its true end; it must aspire to be united with him and to enjoy his presence.

John Nicholas Grou
Meditations on the Love of God

The Word of God, born once in the flesh (such is his kindness and his goodness), is always willing to be born spiritually in those who desire him. In them he is born as an infant as he fashions himself in them by means of their virtues. He reveals himself to the extent that he knows someone is capable of receiving him. He diminishes the revelation of his glory not out of selfishness but because he recognizes the capacity and resources of those who desire to see him. Yet, in the transcendence of mystery, he always remains invisible to all.

St Maximus the Confessor

Poor creature though I be, I am the hand and foot of Christ. I move my hand and my hand is wholly Christ's hand, for deity is become inseparably one with me. I move my foot, and it is aglow with God.

St Symeon the New Theologian

'The kingdom of God is within you' (Luke 17:21). God has just invited us to 'live on in him', to live already, spiritually, in his heritage of glory, now he reveals to us that we need not go outside ourselves to find him. 'The kingdom of God is within you.' St John of the Cross tells us that it is in the substance of the soul, which is inaccessible to both the devil and the world, that God gives himself to us: 'Then all the movements of the soul become divine, and, though they are from God, they are equally from us, because our Lord elicits them in us and with us' (*Living Flame of Love*, v.1). The same saint says elsewhere that God is the 'centre of the soul'. If we know and love God with our whole strength, and find in him our whole joy, we have reached the deepest centre of our being where he is accessible to us. Before arriving at this stage we do already live in God who is the centre of our being but we do not live in our *deepest centre* since we can go further.

As it is love that unites us to God, the more intense our love the deeper we enter into God, and become centred in him. When we possess one degree of love, we are already in our centre, but when this love attains its perfection we will have penetrated into our *deepest centre*. There we will be transformed to the extent of becoming a perfect image of God.

Blessed Elizabeth of the Trinity
Spiritual Writings

In me, in my most interior, Jesus is present. All outside of our heart is only to discover the treasure hidden interiorly in the heart.

There is found that sepulchre of Easter and there the new life. 'Woman, why do you weep? Whom do you seek? Whom you seek, you already possess and you do not know him? You have the true, eternal joy and still you weep? It is more intimate to your being and still you seek it outside! You are there, outside, weeping near the tomb. Your heart is my tomb. And I am not there dead, but I repose there, living always. Your soul is my garden. You are right when you believed that I was the gardener. I am the New Adam. I work and supervise my paradise. Your tears, your love, your desire, all this is my work. You possess me at the most intimate level of your being, without knowing it and this is why you seek me outside. It is then outside also that I appeared to you and also that I make you to return to yourself, to make you find at the intimacy of your being him whom you seek outside.'

A Thirteenth-century Monk
Cited in André Louf's
Teach us to Pray

Every good deed, however small, if it be directed to God by simplicity of intention, increases in us the Divine likeness, and deepens in us the flow of eternal life . . . Entering into and transcending itself, traversing all worlds of being, surpassing all creatures, the soul meets God in its own depths . . . The whole life of the spirit and its activity consists solely in the Divine likeness and this simplicity of intention; and the final peace abides on the heights in simplicity also, in simplicity of essence. Men possess virtues and the Divine likeness in differing measure; in greater or lesser degree have they found their own essence in the depth of themselves, according to their dignity. But God fulfils all; and each, clearer or fainter, according to the measure of his love, possesses the sense of God's presence in the depths of his own being. This contact is Christ's call to the spirit: 'Pass out of thyself, act in the depths.' It invites, attracts, and draws the spirit to that deepest point in its own interior life at which the creature is able to act. Then by the power of love the spirit passes beyond the region of effort into that unity out of whose midst sprang the living flame that touched it.

Jan van Ruysbroeck
Selected works of Ruysbroeck
in *Flowers of a Mystic Garden*
by Ernest Hells

Through Our Daily Life

We must, like him, the Son of God, constantly relate all our activity to the love and the glory of the Father in imitation of the virtues of which he provides the model.

This resemblance to Christ will appear especially in the ever-increasing domination of charity over all our conduct. Love will orient every deliberate action towards our supernatural end; its rays will extend to the whole of our life, and by virtue of its ever-widening sphere of dominion, it will take firmer root in our hearts, and control them in all things. In this manner the kingdom of God becomes more and more firmly established in the Christian soul.

Columba Marmion
Christ the Ideal of the Priest

Love's secret is to be always doing things for God, and not to mind because they are such very little ones.

Frederick William Faber

I come in the little things,
Saith the Lord:
Not borne on morning wings
Of majesty, but I have set my feet
Amidst the delicate and bladed wheat
That springs triumphant in the furrowed sod.
There do I dwell, in weakness and in power;
Not broken or divided, saith our God!
In your strait garden plot I come to flower:
About your porch my vine
Meek, fruitful, doth entwine;
Waits, at the threshold, Love's appointed hour.

I come in the little things,
Saith the Lord:
Yea! on the lancing wings
Of eager birds, the softly pattering feet
Of furred and gentle beasts, I come to meet
Your hard and wayward heart. In brown bright
    eyes
That peep from out the brake, I stand confest.
On every nest
Where feathery Patience is content to brood
And leaves her pleasure for the high emprise
Of motherhood —
There doth my Godhead rest.

I come in the little things,
Saith the Lord:

My starry wings
I do forsake,
Love's highway of humility to take:
Meekly I fit my stature to your need.
In beggar's part
About your gates I shall not cease to plead —
As man, to speak with man —
Till by such art
I shall achieve My Immemorial Plan,
Pass the low lintel of the human heart.

Evelyn Underhill
Innocence

Little things come daily, hourly, within our reach, and they are not less calculated to set forward our growth in holiness, than are the greater occasions which occur but rarely. Moreover, fidelity in trifles, and an earnest seeking to please God in little matters, is a test of real devotion and love. Let your aim be to please our dear Lord perfectly in little things, and to attain a spirit of childlike simplicity and dependence. In proportion as self-love and self-confidence are weakened, and our will bowed to that of God, so will hindrances disappear, the internal troubles and contest which harassed the soul vanish, and it will be filled with peace and tranquillity.

John Nicholas Grou
Manual for Interior Souls

He who is faithful over a few things is a lord of cities. It does not matter whether you preach in Westminster Abbey, or teach a ragged class, so you be faithful. The faithfulness is all.

George MacDonald

Each one of our works, by its more or less remote or direct effect upon the spiritual world, helps to make perfect Christ in his mystical totality. That is the fullest possible answer to the question: How can we, following the call of St Paul, see God in all the active half of our lives? In fact, through the unceasing operation of the Incarnation, the divine so thoroughly permeates all our creaturely energies that, in order to meet it and lay hold on it, we could not find a more fitting setting than that of our action.

To begin with, in action I adhere to the creative power of God; I coincide with it; I become not only its instrument but its living extension. And as there is nothing more personal in a being than his will, I merge myself, in a sense, through my heart, with the very heart of God. This commerce is continuous because I am always acting; and at the same time, since I can never set a boundary to the perfection of my fidelity nor to the fervour of my intention, this commerce enables me to liken myself, ever more strictly and indefinitely, to God.

The soul does not pause to relish this communion, nor does it lose sight of the material end of its action; for it is wedded to a *creative* effort. The will to succeed, a certain passionate delight in the work to be done, form an integral part of our creaturely fidelity. It follows that the very sincerity with which we desire and pursue success for God's sake reveals itself as a new factor – also without limits – in our being knit together with him who animates us. Originally we had fellowship with God in the simple common exercise of wills; but now we unite ourselves with him in the shared love of the end for which we are working; and the crowning marvel is that, with the possession of this end, we have the utter joy of discovering his presence once again.

Pierre Teilhard de Chardin
Le Milieu Divin

Cheered by the presence of God, I will do at each moment, without anxiety, according to the strength which he shall give, the work that his providence assigns me. I will leave the rest without concern; it is not my affair. I ought to consider the duty to which I am called each day, as the work that God has given me to do, and to apply myself to it in a manner worthy of his glory, that is to say, with exactness and in peace. I must neglect nothing; I must be violent about nothing.

François Fenelon
Letters

It is very important for us to realize that God does not lead us all by the same road . . . Remember that there must be someone to cook the meals and count yourselves happy in being able to serve like Martha. Reflect that true humility consists to a great extent in being ready for what the Lord desires to do with you.

Remember that the Lord walks among the pots and pans and that he will help you in the inward tasks and in the outward too.

St Teresa of Avila
The Way of Perfection

Seeing God

All creatures are living in the hand of God; the senses perceive only the action of the creature, but faith sees the action of God in everything – faith believes that Jesus Christ is alive in everything and operates throughout the whole course of the centuries; faith believes that the briefest moment and the tiniest atom contain a portion of Christ's hidden life and his mysterious action. The action of creatures is a veil concealing the profound mysteries of the divine action. Jesus Christ after his resurrection took his disciples by surprise in his apparitions, he presented himself to them under appearances which disguised him; and as soon as he had revealed himself, he disappeared. This very same Jesus, always living and active, still takes by surprise souls whose faith is not sufficiently pure and penetrating.

There is no moment at which God does not present himself under the guise of some suffering, some consolation or some duty. All that occurs within us, around us and by our means covers and hides his divine action. His action is there, most really and certainly present, but in an invisible manner, the result of which is that we are always being taken by surprise and that we only recognize his operation after it has passed. Could we pierce the veil and were we vigilant and attentive, God would reveal himself continuously to us and we should rejoice in his action in everything that happens to us. At every occurrence we should say: *Dominus est.* It is the Lord; and in all circumstances we should find a gift from God: we should consider creatures as very feeble instruments in the hands of an almighty worker, and we should recognize without difficulty that nothing is lacking to us and that God's constant care leads him to give us each instant what is suited to us.

Jean-Pierre de Caussade
Self-Abandonment to
Divine Providence

Imagine a river, or a drop of water, an apple or a grain of sand: God knoweth infinite excellencies in it more than we. He seeth how it relateth to angels and men; how it proceedeth from the most perfect Lover to the most perfectly Beloved; how it representeth all his attributes; how it conduceth in its place, by the best means to the best of ends: and for this cause it cannot be beloved too much. God the Author and God the End is to be beloved in it; Angels and men are to be beloved in it; and it is highly to be esteemed for all their sakes. O what a treasure is every grain of sand when truly understood! Who can love anything that God made too much? What a world would this be, were everything beloved as it ought to be!

Thomas Traherne
Centuries of Meditations

Be with God in thy outward works, refer to him, offer them to him, seek to do them in him and for him, and he will be with thee in them, and they shall not hinder, but rather invite his presence in thy soul. Seek to see him in all things, and in all things he will come nigh to thee.

Edward B. Pusey

102

I hear and behold God in every object, yet understand God
    not in the least,
Nor do I understand who there can be more wonderful than
    myself.
Why should I wish to see God better than this day?
I see something of God each hour of the twenty-four, and
    each moment then,
In the faces of men and women I see God, and in my own
    face in the glass,
I find letters from God dropt in the street, and every one is
    sign'd by God's name,
And I leave them where they are, for I know that wheresoe'er
    I go,
Others will punctually come for ever and ever.

Walt Whitman
Leaves of Grass

Be the dust ne'er so vile, be the motes
    ne'er so small,
The wise man sees God, great and
    glorious, in them all.

Angelus Silesius
*The Spiritual Maxims
of Angelus Silesius*

Reality is charged with a divine Presence. As the mystics
sense and portray it, everything becomes physically and
literally lovable in God; and reciprocally God becomes
knowable and lovable in all that surrounds us. In the
greatness and depths of its cosmic stuff, in the maddening
number of elements and events which compose it, and in the

fullness of the general currents which dominate and set it in motion like a great wave, the World, filled with God, no longer appears to our opened eyes as anything but a milieu and an object of universal communion.

Pierre Teilhard de Chardin

I see his blood upon the rose
And in the stars the glory of his eyes,
His body gleams amid eternal snows,
His tears fall from the skies.

I see his face in every flower;
The thunder and the singing of the birds
Are but his voice – and carven by his power
Rocks are his written words.

All pathways by his feet are worn,
His strong heart stirs the ever-beating sea,
His crown of thorns is twined with every thorn,
His cross is every tree.

Joseph Mary Plunkett

Chapter Six

Prayer

Prayer

I take it for granted that every Christian that is in health is up early in the morning, for it is much more reasonable to suppose a person up early because he is a Christian than because he is a labourer, or a tradesman, or a servant, or has business that wants him.

We naturally conceive some abhorrence of a man that is in bed when he should be at his labour or in his shop. We cannot tell how to think anything good of him who is such a slave to drowsiness as to neglect his business for it.

Let this therefore teach us to conceive how odious we must appear in the sight of heaven if we are in bed, shut up in sleep and darkness, when we should be praising God, and all such slaves to drowsiness as to neglect our devotions for it.

For if he is to be blamed as a slothful drone that rather chooses the lazy indulgence of sleep than to perform his proper share of worldly business, how much more is he to be reproached that would rather be folded up in a bed than be raising up his heart to God in acts of praise and adoration!

Prayer is the nearest approach to God, and the highest enjoyment of him, that we are capable of in this life.

It is the noblest exercise of the soul, the most exalted use of our best faculties and the highest imitation of the blessed inhabitants of heaven.

When our hearts are full of God, sending up holy desires to the throne of grace, we are then in our highest state, we are upon the utmost heights of human greatness; we are not before kings and princes, but in the presence and audience of the Lord of all the world, and can be no higher till death is swallowed up in glory.

William Law
A Serious Call to a Devout Life

To lift up the hands in prayer gives God glory, but a man with a dung-fork in his hand, a woman with a slop-pail, give him glory, too. He is so great that all things give him glory if you mean they should.

Gerard Manley Hopkins
Letters

Prayer means turning to reality, taking our part, however humble, tentative and half-understood, in the continual conversation, the communion, of our spirits with the Eternal Spirit; the acknowledgement of our entire dependence, which is yet the partly free dependence of the child. For prayer is really our whole life toward God: our longing for him, our 'incurable God-sickness', as Barth calls it, our whole drive towards him. It is the humble correspondence of the human spirit with the sum of all perfection, the fountain of life. No narrower definition than this is truly satisfactory, or covers all the ground.

Evelyn Underhill
The Spiritual Life

He (the Christian) will pray in every place, but not openly to be seen of men. He prays in every situation, in his walks for recreation, in his intercourse with others, in silence, in reading, in all rational pursuits. And although he is only thinking of God in the little chamber of the soul, and calling upon his Father with silent aspirations, God is near him and with him while he is yet speaking.

St Clement of Alexandria
The Instructor

So have I seen a lark rising from its bed of grass, and soaring upwards, singing as he rises, and hopes to get to heaven and climb above the clouds; but the poor bird was beaten back with the loud sighings of an eastern wind, and his motion made irregular and inconstant, descending more at every breath of the tempest than it could recover by the liberation and frequent weighing of his wings; till the little creature was forced to sit down and pant, and stay till the storm was over; and then it made a prosperous flight, and did rise and sing, as if it had learned music and motion from an angel, as he passed sometimes through the air, about his ministries here below: so is the prayer of a good man.

Jeremy Taylor
The Return of Prayers (Part II)

Understanding prayer well means understanding that one is speaking with God.

Thus there are two poles. One very, very tiny and very, very weak: my soul. One immense and powerful: God.

But here is the first paradox, the first surprise: that he who is so great should have wanted to speak to me, tiny as I am.

It is not I who wanted prayer. It is he who wanted it. It is not I who have looked for him. It is he who has looked for me first. My seeking him would have been in vain if before all time he had not sought me.

The hope on which my prayer rests is in the fact that it is he who wants it. And if I go to keep the appointment it is because he is already there waiting for me.

Carlo Carretto
Letters from the Desert

All who call on God in true faith, earnestly from the heart, will certainly be heard, and will receive what they have asked and desired, although not in the hour or in the measure, or the very thing which they ask; yet they will obtain something greater and more glorious than they had dared to ask.

Martin Luther

'Be sober and watch because your adversary, the Devil, as a roaring lion goeth about seeking whom he may devour' (1 Peter 5:8). Watch, that is to say, be vigilant in prayer. Now what sort of prayer had St Peter in mind? Not prayer of words (which some people, for instance, those who say over numberless psalms, call prayer exclusively), but that which our Lord meant when he said that true worshippers worship in spirit and in truth. The saints and teachers of the Church tell us that prayer is a lifting-up of the mind to God. Reading and vocal prayer help in this lifting-up, and it is good to use them for this purpose; just as my clothes are useful to me, but are not me, so spoken words are a help to true prayer without being that prayer: its essence is that the heart and mind go out to God without intermediary. True prayer is simply that, and nothing else: the lifting-up of the mind to

God in love, interior longing for and humble submission to him.

Clergy are bound to the recitation of the Divine Office, but no prayer is so full of love and worship as the sacred Our Father which our sovereign master Christ himself taught to us, and it conduces to true essential prayer better than any other. It is a heavenly prayer, which the blessed sing and meditate upon without ceasing.

St Augustine says that there is a mysterious place deep in the soul that is beyond time and this world, a part higher than that which gives life and movement to the body; true prayer so raises the heart that God can come into this innermost place, the most disinterested, intimate and noble part of our being, the seat of our unity. It is his eternal dwelling-place, and into this grand mysterious kingdom he pours the sweet delight of which I have spoken. Then is man no longer troubled by anything: he is recollected, quiet, and really himself, and becomes daily more detached, spiritualized, and contemplative, for God is within him, reigning and working in the depths of his soul. This spiritual state of man cannot be compared with what has gone before, for he has now taken on a Divine life; the spirit is set in God, drowned in that fire of charity which is essentially and of its nature God himself.

John Tauler
Sermons of John Tauler

Since prayer opens our mind to the brightness of divine light and our will to the warmth of heavenly love, nothing so purges our mind of ignorance and our will of evil desires.

St Francis of Sales
Introduction to the Devout Life

Man has a noble task: that of prayer and love. To pray and to love, that is the happiness of man on earth.

Prayer is nothing else than union with God. When the heart is pure and united with God it is consoled and filled with sweetness; it is dazzled by a marvellous light. In this intimate union God and the soul are like two pieces of wax moulded into one; they cannot any more be separated. It is a very wonderful thing, this union of God with his insignificant creature, a happiness passing all understanding.

St Jean-Baptiste Vianney
Instructions

When the members of Christ pray, they shall not separate from the head . . . God's Son alone shall plead for us, and plead within us, and be implored by us . . . He himself is the pleader in our midst.

St Augustine of Hippo

To persist in prayer without returns, this is not time lost, but a great gain. It is endeavour without thought of self and only for the glory of the Lord. Even though at first it seems that the effort is all in vain, it is not so, but it is as with children who work in their father's fields: they receive no daily wage, but when the year comes to an end, everything belongs to them . . .

He who sets out to pray must be as the husbandman. In the season of summer and fair weather he (as the ant) must not grow weary, so that he may be fed in the season of winter and stormy rains. He must have a full larder so that he may live and not (like the dumb beasts) die of hunger. For we must be prepared for the great storm of death and judgement.

In Albula I learned to know a certain saint who lived as it is fitting for a saint. After she had given away all for the sake of the Lord, she had left a cover to protect her from the cold, and this she gave also. Soon after this, God afflicted her with the greatest inner pain and a feeling of loneliness. Whereat she complained and said to him: 'Is this meet, dear Lord? You have taken all from me, and now you yourself forsake me too!'

Here, then, God repaid the great services performed for him, with sorrow. And there can, indeed, be no better payment, for the true meaning of it is that one is paid with the love of God.

Do not let your heart cling to inner solace. For that is in the manner of common soldiers: they demand their daily wage at once. Give your service as the noblest officers serve their king – for nothing!

St Teresa of Avila
The Interior Castle

The Lord's Prayer

Whatever particular object we may want to pray for, we have never prayed for it aright till we have prayed for it in the words and spirit of the Lord's Prayer. That is not one prayer among many. It covers all legitimate Christian praying, and indeed the saying of it affords the best tests whether our wants of the moment can become a prayer offered 'in the name of Christ'.

I say 'in the name of Christ'. The Lord's Prayer is the great prayer in his name. You know how many people have a very strangely childish notion, that praying in the name of Christ means simply the addition of the words 'through Jesus Christ our Lord' at the end of their prayers. But depend upon it, they do not by adding these words, or any words, bring it about that their prayers should be in the name of Christ. To pray in the name of Christ means to pray in such a way as represents Christ. The representative always must speak in the spirit and meaning of those for whom he speaks. If Christ is our representative, that must be because he speaks our wishes, or what we ought to make our wishes; and if we are to pray in the name of Christ, that means that we are, however far off, expressing his wishes and intentions.

Therefore, as the Lord's Prayer represents profoundly and perfectly the spirit of him who first spoke it, and who taught it to his Church, it follows that it is, beyond all other prayers, the prayer in Christ's name. Do you then want to know whether this or that thing can be prayed for in Christ's name? The answer is to be found in another question. Can it be legitimately covered by the clauses of the Lord's Prayer?

Bishop Gore
Sermon on the Mount

The Lord's Prayer is the prayer above all prayers. It is a prayer which the most high Master taught us, wherein are comprehended all spiritual and temporal blessings, and the strongest comforts in all trials, temptations and troubles, even in the hour of death.

Martin Luther

The sublime perfection of this evangelical prayer is marvellous and we ought to thank God fervently for it. So admirably is it composed by the good Master that everybody may apply its meaning to his own wants. I am astonished at finding all perfection and contemplation comprised in so few words that there seems to be no need to study any book but this. For so far our Lord has taught the whole mode of prayer and high contemplation from the beginning to mental prayer, quietude and union, so that if I could express myself, I could write a large book on prayer built on such a trustworthy foundation.

St Teresa of Avila
The Way of Perfection

Last summer, doing Greek with T . . . I went through the Our Father word for word in Greek. We promised each other to learn it by heart. I do not think he ever did so, but some weeks later, as I was turning over the pages of the Gospel, I said to myself that since I had promised to do this thing and it was good, I ought to do it. I did it. The infinite sweetness of this Greek text so took hold of me that for several days I could not stop myself from saying it over all the time. A week afterward I began the vine harvest. I recited the Our Father in Greek every day before work, and I repeated it very often in the vineyard.

Since that time I have made a practice of saying it through once each morning with absolute attention. If during the recitation my attention wanders or goes to sleep, in the minutest degree, I begin again, until I have once succeeded in going through it with absolutely pure attention. Sometimes it comes about that I say it again out of sheer pleasure, but I only do it if I really feel the impulse.

The effect of this practice is extraordinary, and surprises me every time, for, although I experience it each day, it exceeds my expectation at each repetition.

At times the very first words tear my thoughts from my body and transport it to a place outside space where there is neither perspective nor point of view. The infinity of the ordinary expanses of perception is replaced by an infinity to the second or sometimes the third degree. At the same time, filling every part of this infinity of infinity, there is silence, a silence which is not an absence of sound but which is the object of a positive sensation, more positive than that of sound. Noises, if there are any, only reach me after crossing this silence.

Sometimes, also, during this recitation or at other moments, Christ is present with me in person, but his presence is infinitely more real, more moving, more clear than on that first occasion when he took possession of me.

Simone Weil
Waiting on God

What deep mysteries, my dearest brothers, are contained in the Lord's Prayer! How many and great they are! They are expressed in a few words but they are rich in spiritual power so that nothing is left out; every petition and prayer we have to make is included. It is a compendium of heavenly doctrine.

St Cyprian
De dominica oratione

Every day we plead in the Lord's Prayer, 'Thy will be done!', yet when his will is done we grumble and are not pleased with it.

Meister Eckhart
Sermons

Is it possible to call God *our Father* from a heart that is not full of the feeling that the very name evokes? Can we have the affection a son should have for such a Father, if we have not given ourselves entirely to him? Ponder well on all the duties that respect, love, gratitude and dependence impose on us in his regard, as his creatures and children by adoption. Judge for yourself whether your first and most indispensable duty is not to give your heart wholly and irrevocably to him.

Now in the Lord's Prayer the first thing we ask is that his name shall be hallowed: that is to say, that all the glory due to this ineffable name may be rendered to it. But rendered by whom? By all creatures, but most of all by ourselves. All our life, then, ought to be a continuous honouring of his holy name, a continual longing that it may be similarly honoured by others. Zeal for his glory should burn in our hearts and consume them when we behold all the outrages by which that name is dishonoured, and the gift of our heart is the only way in which this can become a reality to us. If there are so few Christians who feel like this, it is because so few have made a complete oblation of their heart to God. And what is this glory that he expects from us? That of being loved in all and above all things. 'God', says St Augustine, 'is only honoured by love.' All his commandments are reduced to and comprised in love. And what is love but the gift to God of our heart and all that this implies?

In the second place, we ask in the Lord's Prayer that his kingdom may come. What is this kingdom? It is that of our love. And where would he establish it? In our hearts. It is true that this kingdom will only be perfected in heaven, but it must commence on earth. And how can it begin in any of us except by the gift of our heart? God only reigns in us in the measure in which he is master of our will; and he has control over our affections only in so far as they are reduced to one love only, of which he is the object. His kingdom is only established when self-love, his chief enemy, is totally destroyed. And it is only by giving our heart to him without reserve that our resolution to banish self-love completely becomes really effective. We do this first by our own efforts, seconded always by grace, and then by allowing God to give self-love its death-blow.

We then go on to ask that the will of God may be done on earth as it is done in heaven. Is this not the same thing as asking that my heart may belong to him as perfectly as the hearts of the Blessed in heaven? That he may find no more resistance to *his* good pleasure on my part than on theirs? That I may be filled with the same zeal, the same spirit of obedience, the same disinterestedness in carrying out the least of his commands? If this is not my intention when I recite this petition, it is certain that I am not fulfilling our Lord's intentions, and that I am not sincere in my prayer to our heavenly Father. I pronounce the words with my lips, but they do not come from the heart. And how can they unless my heart is completely his? These petitions, so holy in themselves, do not ring true as I say them, so long as I refuse him what he asks for from me for the hallowing of his name, for the coming of his kingdom, and for the perfect fulfilment of his will. I must examine myself seriously on this point, and until I have made an entire oblation of myself to him, I may have grave reason to fear that I may well be saying this prayer to my condemnation.

John Nicholas Grou
Meditations on the Love of God

'Our Father, who art in heaven.' We must seek him and above all dwell with him in this little heaven he has made for himself in the centre of our soul. Christ once told the Samaritan woman that: 'The Father claims for his worshippers such men as will worship him in spirit, and in truth.' To give joy to his heart, let us be these true worshippers. Let us worship him *in spirit*, that is with heart and mind fixed on him and with our spirit enlightened by the knowledge of him afforded by faith. Let us adore him *in truth*, that is by our actions which prove our sincerity when we do always what pleases the Father, whose children we are.

Blessed Elizabeth of the Trinity
Spiritual Writings

Practice of the Presence of God

I think you should try, without any painful effort, to dwell upon God as often as a longing for recollection, and regret that you cannot cultivate it more, comes over you. It will not do to wait for disengaged seasons, when you can close your door and be alone. The moment in which we crave after recollection is that in which to practise it; turn your heart then and there to God, simply, familiarly and trustfully. The most interrupted seasons may be used thus; not merely when you are out driving, but when you are dressing, having your hair arranged – even when you are eating, and when others are talking. Useless and tiresome details in conversation will afford you similar opportunities; instead of wearying you, or exciting your ridicule, they will give you time for recollection; and thus all things turn to good for those who love God.

François Fenelon
Letter to the Comtesse de Gramont

One way to recall easily the mind in time of prayer, and to preserve it more in rest, is not to let it wander too far at other times. You should keep it strictly in the Presence of God, and being accustomed to think of him often from time to time, you will find it easy to keep your mind calm in the time of prayer, or at least to recall it from its wanderings.

Brother Lawrence
The Practice of the Presence of God

'Having found in many books, different methods of going to God, and divers practices of the spiritual life, I thought this would serve rather to puzzle me, than facilitate what I sought after, which was nothing but how to become wholly God's . . . I renounced for the love of him everything that was not he; and I began to live as though there was none but he and I in the world . . . I worshipped him the oftenest that I could, keeping my mind in his holy Presence, and recalling it as often as I found it wandered from him. I found no small pain in this exercise, and yet I continued it notwithstanding all the difficulties that occurred . . . or disquieting myself . . . I made this my business, as much all the day long as at the appointed times of prayer . . . and though I have done it very imperfectly, yet have I found great advantages by it . . .

When we are faithful to keep ourselves in his holy Presence, and set him always before us; this not only hinders our offending him . . . at least wilfully, but it also begets holy freedom, and if I may so speak, a familiarity with God where with we ask . . . the graces we stand in need of.

Brother Lawrence
The Practice of the Presence of God

It is by frequent raising of my mind and heart to God as to their proper object that the practice of the presence of God becomes easy, and that the love of God increases and is strengthened in my soul. Then will I realize what St Augustine meant when he said: 'God is closer to us than we are to ourselves', and: 'I sought you outside of me, and all the while you were within me' (*Confessions*).

And this way of loving God, the loveliest and easiest of all, is at the same time also the most efficacious, because it need never be interrupted. There is nothing to prevent my mind and my heart being raised to God, and what we do often cannot fail in time to produce a noticeable effect. Moreover, the more one thinks of an object such as God, the more lovable he becomes; and the more one loves the more one wants to love. Thus the practice of the presence of God, being an exercise of love, is bound to result in an increase of love.

John Nicholas Grou
Meditations on the Love of God

Brother Lawrence had found such an advantage in walking in the presence of God, it was natural for him to recommend it earnestly to others; but his example was a stronger

119

inducement than any arguments he could propose. His very countenance was edifying; such a sweet and calm devotion appearing in it, as could not but affect the beholders. And it was observed, that in the greatest hurry of business in the kitchen, he still preserved his recollection and heavenly-mindedness. He was never hasty nor loitering, but did each thing in its season, with an even uninterrupted composure and tranquillity of spirit. 'The time of business', said he, 'does not with me differ from the time of prayer; and in the noise and clatter of my kitchen, while several persons are at the same time calling for different things, I possess God in as great tranquillity as if I were upon my knees at the Blessed Sacrament.'

The Practice of the Presence of God
(Letters and Conversations of
Brother Lawrence)

Whoever does not have God truly within himself, but is remote from God, so that he must always fetch him from the outside, from here and there, and seeks him in different ways, in a deed, or in a person, or in a place, he does not have God.

The true having of God is a matter of the heart and of the intrinsic and conscious turning and striving to God, and certainly not of an even and constant thought of God. For to accomplish this would be impossible for the nature of man, and would be too difficult, and not even best. For man shall not merely think of God and let this suffice. When the thought vanishes, God vanishes also. But man shall be filled with the essence of God that is high above the thought of man, and above all things created. *That* God cannot vanish, unless man turn from him voluntarily.

Whoever is thus filled with the essence of God grasps his Godhood, and God shines out to him in all things. For all things will seem to him related to God and God will appear to him in all things. God is awake within him at all times. He quietly turns from the outside world and God who is present, God, the Beloved, invades him. Just as one who is burning with thirst, with a real thirst, may do other things than drink, and may even think of other things, but whatever he may do or with whomever he may be, with whatever wishes or thoughts, or whatever doing, he never fails to see the draught before him as long as he thirsts, and the greater his thirst, the greater and more intrinsic and intense and constant is his vision of the draught. And whoever loves something fervently and with all his strength, so that nothing but this delights him and touches his heart, so that he wants only this and nothing else, verily, wherever or with whomever he may be, or whatever he plans or does, he will never forget what he so loves, and in all things he will see the image of the One, and he will see it within him more clearly as his love grows deeper and deeper. Such a man does not seek rest, for he is not confused by any unrest.

Such a man is all the more the recipient of God's grace, in that to him all things are replete with God and more than just the things in themselves. But this, indeed, requires zeal and devotion and incessant care of our inner life, and a keen and clear and deep awareness that determines the response of the heart to me and to things. And man cannot learn this through flight, by fleeing from things and turning to solitude away from all that is without, but he must acquire an inner solitude, no matter where or with whom he may be. He must learn to break through the shell of things and to grasp God therein, and to use all his power to shape God within himself to an image that does not fade.

Just like one who wants to learn to write! If he would master this skill he must practise much and often, no matter how difficult and tedious this may be or how impossible it may seem. If he only practises much and industriously he will learn and master this skill. First he must think of every letter separately and seize upon it firmly with his imagination. But when he has mastered the skill, he can give up imagining and thinking of the separate letters. He will write freely and easily, whether it be trivialities or bold thoughts that he would express by his skill. Now it is sufficient for him to know that he must use his skill, and even though he does not think of it continually, indeed, no matter what he may be thinking of, through his skills he accomplishes his work.

Thus shall man also be pervaded with the presence of God and shaped by the shape of his beloved God, and be so fused with him that God is present within him and shines within him without any effort on his part, and that he recognizes the true nature of all things and remains free from them. But to attain to this, he must first concentrate his thought and deliberately learn as a student learns his skill.

Meister Eckhart
Sermons

Chapter Seven

In Simplicity

Simplicity

O God, how soon we shall be in eternity! There we shall know how little it has to do with all the affairs of this world, and how little it matters whether we succeeded in them or not. And yet now we trouble ourselves about them as though they were, heaven knows, how important! When we were little children how busily we fetched pieces of brick and wood and clay to build a little house or a hut. And if someone had broken it up, how we wept! But now we know very well that all this trumpery was of small account. The same will come to pass in heaven when we know that all the troubles of this world were only childish matters. And yet I would not set aside all care for these fripperies, for God has assigned them to us so that we may practise our soul; but I should like to remove from this care all passion and violence. Let us be childish, since we are children! But let us not catch cold in so being, and if someone comes and breaks up our little house and crosses our plans, let us not be too grieved thereat. But when the evening comes that brings us rest, when death approaches, then the little house does not matter at all. For then we must enter the house of our Father. So attend faithfully to your affairs, but be assured that there is no affair as important as that of your salvation and that nothing is so necessary for your salvation as that you keep your soul on the path that leads to true blessedness in God.

St Francis of Sales
Introduction to a Devout Life

I've always wished that I could be a saint. But whenever I compared myself to the Saints there was always this unfortunate difference – they were like great mountains, hiding their heads in the clouds, and I was only an insignificant grain of sand, trodden down by all who passed by. However, I wasn't going to be discouraged; I said to myself: 'God wouldn't inspire us with ambitions that can't be realized. Obviously there's nothing great to be made of me, so it must be possible for me to aspire to sanctity in spite of my insignificance. I've got to take myself just as I am, with all my imperfections; but somehow I shall have to find out a little way, all of my own, which will be a direct short-cut to heaven. After all [I said to myself] we live in an age of inventions. Nowadays, people don't even bother to climb the stairs – rich people, anyhow; they find a lift more convenient. Can't I find a lift which will take me up to Jesus, since I'm not big enough to climb the steep stairway of perfection?' So I looked in the Bible for some hint about the lift I wanted, and I came across the passage where Eternal Wisdom says: 'Is anyone simple as a little child? Then let him come to me.' To that Wisdom I went; it seemed as if I was on the right track; what did God undertake to do for the child-like soul that responded to his invitation? I read on, and this is what I found: 'I will console you like a mother caressing her son; you shall be like children carried at the breast, fondled on a mother's lap' (Isaiah 66:12,13). Never were words so touching: never was such music to rejoice the heart – I could, after all, be lifted up to heaven, in the arms of Jesus! And if that was to happen, there was no need for me to grow bigger; on the contrary, I must be as small as ever, smaller than ever.

St Thérèse of Lisieux
Autobiography of a Saint

Love needs to be proved by action. Well, even a little child can scatter flowers, to scent the throne-room with their fragrance; even a little child can sing, in its shrill treble, the great canticle of Love. That shall be my life, to scatter flowers – to miss no single opportunity of making some small sacrifice, here by a smiling look, there by a kindly word, always doing the tiniest thing right, and doing it for love. I shall suffer all that I have to suffer – yes, and enjoy all my enjoyments too – in the spirit of love, so that I shall always be scattering flowers before your throne; nothing that comes my way but shall yield up its petals in your honour. And, as I scatter my flowers, I shall be singing; how could one be sad when occupied so pleasantly? I shall be singing, even when I have to pluck my flowers from a thorn-bush; never in better voice than when the thorns are longest and sharpest. I don't ask what use they will be to us, Jesus, these flowers, this music of mine, I know that you will take pleasure in this fragrant shower of worthless petals, in these songs of love in which a worthless heart like mine sings itself out. And because they will give pleasure to you, the Church triumphant in heaven will smile upon them too; will take these flowers so bruised by love and pass them on into your divine hands. And so the Church in heaven, ready to take part in the childish game I am playing, will begin scattering these flowers, now hallowed by your touch beyond all recognition.

St Thérèse of Lisieux
Autobiography of a Saint

There are souls among those whom God leads by this way of simplicity, whom his divine goodness strips so extra-ordinarily of all satisfaction, desire and feeling that they had difficulty in enduring and in expressing themselves, because what passes in their interior life is so slight, so delicate and so imperceptible, being all at the extreme summit of the spirit, that they do not know how to speak of it. And these souls sometimes suffer greatly if their superiors are not acquainted with their way, because, fearing to be useless and to be wasting time, they wish to achieve something, and rack their brains with reflections, so as to be able to observe what is going on within them; this is very prejudicial to them, and causes them to fall into great perplexities of mind which are difficult to unravel, unless they submit to discard these reflections entirely and to suffer with patience the pain that they feel – which pain is often due merely to their always wishing to be doing something, and not being content with what they have, and this disturbs their peace of mind and causes them to lose that very simple and very delicate interior occupation of their will.

St Jane Frances de Chantal

He to whom all things are one, he who reduceth all things to one, and seeth all things in one, may enjoy a quiet mind, and remain peaceable in God.

Thomas à Kempis
The Imitation of Christ

The soul, by the simplicity of the gaze she fixes on her divine object, is separated from all about her, separated above all from self, and then the shining of the light within her 'makes known his glory as he revealed it in the features of Jesus Christ' (2 Corinthians 4:6).

Blessed Elizabeth of the Trinity
Spiritual Writings

Silence

I do not know when I have had happier times in my soul, than when I have been sitting at work, with nothing before me but a candle and a white cloth, and hearing no sound but that of my own breath, with God in my soul and heaven in my eye . . . I rejoice in being exactly what I am – a creature capable of loving God, and who, as long as God lives must be happy. I get up and look for a while out of the window, and gaze at the moon and stars, the work of an Almighty hand. I think of the grandeur of the universe, and then sit down, and think myself one of the happiest beings in it.

A Poor Methodist Woman
(Eighteenth Century)

Elected Silence, sing to me
And beat upon my whorled ear,
Pipe me to pastures still and be
The music that I care to hear.

Shape nothing, lips; be lovely dumb:
It is the shut, the curfew sent
From there where all surrenders come
Which only makes you eloquent.

Be shelled, eyes, with double dark
And find the uncreated light:
This ruck and reel which you remark
Coils, keeps and teases simple sight.

Palate, the hutch of tasty lust,
Desire not to be rinsed with wine:
The can must be so sweet, the crust
So fresh that come in feasts divine!

Gerard Manley Hopkins

Then we discover what the spiritual life really is . . . It is the
silence of our whole being in compunction and adoration
before God, in the habitual realization that he is everything
and we are nothing, that he is the centre to which all things
tend, and to whom all our actions must be directed. That
our life and strength proceed from him, that both in life and
in death we depend entirely on him.

Thomas Merton
Thoughts in Solitude

The speech of created beings is with sounds. The word of
God is silence. God's secret world of love can be nothing else
but silence.

Simone Weil
Waiting on God

When I set myself sometimes to consider the divers agitations of men, and the troubles and dangers to which they expose themselves . . . I see that all their misfortunes come from one thing only, that they know not how to dwell in peace, in a room.

Blaise Pascal
Les Pensées

In order to listen well, silence is needful; it is needful that we should often, like Jesus at the Transfiguration, go apart into a solitary place. Certainly Jesus is to be found elsewhere, even in the turmoil of great cities, but he is only heard well in a peaceful soul surrounded by an atmosphere of silence. He is only understood in a soul that prays. It is then above all that he reveals himself to the soul, drawing her to him and transfiguring her in him.

Columba Marmion
Christ in His Mysteries

There is hardly ever a complete silence in our soul. God is whispering to us wellnigh incessantly. Whenever the sounds of the world die out in the soul, or sink low, then we hear these whisperings of God. He is always whispering to us, only we do not always hear, because of the noise, hurry and distraction which life causes as it rushes on.

Frederick William Faber
Sermons

'Rest in the Lord; wait patiently for him.' In Hebrew, 'be silent to God, and let him mould thee.' Keep still, and he will mould thee to the right shape.

Martin Luther

God is a tranquil being, and abides in a tranquil eternity. So must thy spirit become a tranquil and clear little pool, wherein the serene light of God can be mirrored.

Gerhard Tersteegen
Sermons

My rule tells me: 'Your strength will be in silence.' I think then that to keep one's strength for the Lord is to unify one's whole being by interior silence; it is to recollect all one's powers in order to engage in the single work of love; it is to have that clear eye which allows the divine light to illuminate us.

Blessed Elizabeth of the Trinity
Spiritual Writings

Detachment

God ordered Isaiah to strip himself naked (Isaiah 20:2,3). This the prophet did, and went about preaching like that for three whole days, according to some commentators – three years, according to others. At last when the time prefixed by God expired, he put on his clothes again. In the same way we are to strip ourselves of all attachments, little or great; we are frequently to examine our consciences to see if we are ready, as Isaiah was, to divest ourselves of all our garments. Then we too, when the time comes, are to take up again such inclinations as are suited to charity's service. Thus we shall be able to die naked with our Saviour on the cross, to rise again with him in newness of life (Romans 6:4–6). *Not death itself is so strong as love* (Cant. 8:6), to make us release our hold on everything; and charity is sublime as the resurrection to adorn us with grandeur and glory.

St Francis of Sales
The Love of God

Perhaps few things are more misunderstood than this idea of detachment. People sometimes think that it means not caring: it does, but, as we have seen, only if you add that it means caring too. The detached man will care more for things than the avaricious and rapacious man; but he will care in a different way. He will not clutch and cling, in self-worship; his possessions, his desires, his attachments, will not fetter his freedom and destroy his power of love, will not forever be an anxiety and an agitation of spirit. His is the prayer of the poet,

> Teach us to care and not to care.
> Teach us to sit still

and so he learns to be at peace.

The first thing is to care: it is precisely what the rapacious man does not do. We cannot help wanting things; it is our nature; but what makes the difference is how we want, and how we express our want. Things are not just means; they are God's handiwork, lovely in themselves, therefore, and to

131

be treated with reverence. And they are one with us in the unity of God's family; and so they are to be treated with love. And they are his creatures and not ours, and so they are to be used or enjoyed – they are to become possessions – only within the framework of his will. You do no harm to God or to things or to yourself if you use them or enjoy them according to their nature and his will for you, provided your attitude is one of love and reverence, provided you have first learnt to see and love and serve, provided you have learnt to care. We lose the power to love and enjoy things as we should when we lose the power of vision; and we lose the power of vision when we lose the life of the child . . .

But then if you care like this you learn also not to care. If you learn to see God in all things you will learn to love them according to his will, not your own self-will. If you see things as in eternity you are less a prey to the pain of their passing, and so you can learn the more easily not to clutch at them as they pass. If you see God in all things and all things in God you learn to be reverent and not proudly possessive. And where it is a question of legitimate possession and legitimate use – and these are measured by the end that God has set for you, your manner of life and the work you do and the needs of your *being* – then you will learn the more easily not to sin by excess or superfluity, nor to hold fast at all costs when God would take from you what he has given: you will learn the more easily not to care.

Gerald Vann
The Divine Pity

Liberty of spirit consists not at all in being more free with God or less anxious in the discharge of our spiritual duties, but in this single thing, detachment from creatures. Liberty and detachment are one and the same thing. He is free who is detached, and he only. But it is plain that no one can be detached who is not generous also; for generosity consists in detaching ourselves, always at cost and with pain, from creatures for the sake of the Creator.

Frederick William Faber
Growth in Holiness

In order to arrive at possessing everything,
   Desire to possess nothing.
In order to arrive at being everything,
   Desire to be nothing.
In order to arrive at knowing everything,
   Desire to know nothing.
In order to arrive at that wherein thou hast no pleasure,
   Thou must go by a way wherein thou hast no
      pleasure.
In order to arrive at that which thou knowest not,
   Thou must go by a way that thou knowest not.
In order to arrive at that which thou possessest not,
   Thou must go by a way that thou possessest not.
In order to arrive at that which thou art not,
   Thou must go through that which thou art not.

St John of the Cross
Ascent of Mount Carmel

As we grow in holiness our attachments to creatures weaken, and those that remain riveted are riveted in God. It is not that sanctity lies in unfeelingness. Look at St Francis de Sales stretched on the floor of the room where his mother has just died, and sobbing as if his heart was broken. Strong angels look at the prostrate saint without upbraiding; for his grief is a human holiness rather than a human weakness. Not for a moment, said he, in all that tempest of grief was his will removed one line's breadth from the sweet sovereign will of God. All that is irregular, earthly, and inordinate in our attachments fades out. Nay, we are sensibly conscious to ourselves of an actual decay of all strong feelings, of whatever kind, in our hearts; and the absence of these is rest; for strong earthly feelings are a tyranny.

Secondly, we have now no worldly end in view; and thus there is nothing proximate to disquiet us. What success can we have to look forward to? Is it a point in riches we would fain reach? Or a summit on which an ambitious imagination has often placed us in our daydreams? Or a scheme that we are burning to realize? Such things belong not to the spiritual. They know nothing of them; except that they have been burned by them in former times. They have scathed them, and passed on. Not even works of mercy now can be ends of themselves, ends in which to rest. They are but stepping-stones we lay down for God's glory and his angels to pass over the earth and bless its misery. There may be rest in straining to a supernatural end, or the very strain may be more welcome than the most luxurious rest. But there can be no rest for those who are straining after a worldly end, blameless even if perchance it be.

Thirdly, holiness brings us rest, because it delivers us even from spiritual ambition, in any of its various forms. As I have already said, the inordinate pursuit of virtue is itself a vice, and the anxious desire to be speedily rid of all our imperfections is a delusion of self-love.

Frederick William Faber
Growth in Holiness

Too often people imagine that Christian detachment consists in loving nothing. This is terribly wrong. Never has there been a heart more loving than the heart of Jesus, and our hearts should be modelled on his. To love is the great, indeed the only, commandment. *This is the first commandment . . . thou shalt love the Lord thy God with thy whole heart . . . and thy neighbour*. There you have the whole Gospel, the whole of life, the whole of God, who is love itself. Love, yes: but an ordered love, which is a living and communicating force, capable of immolating everything that prevents it from giving itself.

And this immolation to love of all that is not love is what we call detachment. Detachment, then, is the negative side of attachment (or love). It is detachment which 'sets in order' our loves. *Ordinavit in me caritatem . . .* He has *set in order* charity in me. The God of Love, living in a soul, causes it to love all other beings, in so far as they participate in him, who is being. The soul must love them as God loves them – that is to say, in the same way as God gives himself to them. It is this gift of Infinite Being to a finite being that gives it life, and is the measure of our love. Our love, measured by God himself and by what we find of him in his works, is an ordered love. This being so, there must be no attachments which are not in conformity with this rule. If the soul finds any such within itself, it does not suppress them, it disciplines them. This idea of order is at the root of everything. Detachment is the condition of order, just as order is the condition of love. And that is why it can be said that detachment is 'ordered love'.

A Carthusian
They Speak by Silences

Chapter Eight

The Will of God

God's Will

St Paul did not want to be an apostle to the Gentiles. He wanted to be a clever and appreciated young Jewish scholar, and kicked against the pricks. St Ambrose and St Augustine did not want to be overworked and worried bishops. Nothing was farther from their intention. St Cuthbert wanted the solitude and freedom of his hermitage on the Farne; but he did not often get there. St Francis Xavier's preference was for an ordered life close to his beloved master, St Ignatius. At a few hours' notice he was sent out to be the Apostle of the Indies and never returned to Europe again. Henry Martyn, the fragile and exquisite scholar, was compelled to sacrifice the intellectual life to which he was so perfectly fitted for the missionary life to which he felt he was decisively called. In all these, a power beyond themselves decided the direction of life. Yet in all we recognize not frustration, but the highest of all types of achievement. Things like this – and they are constantly happening – gradually convince us that the over-ruling reality of life is the Will and Choice of a Spirit acting not in a mechanical but in a living and personal way; and that the spiritual life of man does not consist in mere individual betterment, or assiduous attention to his own soul, but in a free and unconditional response to that Spirit's pressure and call, whatever the cost may be.

Evelyn Underhill
The Spiritual Life

'Yes, heavenly Father, I accept everything, yes, and always yes.'

St Francis of Sales

Your external circumstances may change, toil may take the place of rest, sickness of health, trials may thicken within and without. Externally, you are the prey of such circumstances; but if your heart is stayed on God, no changes or chances can touch it, and all that may befall you will but draw you closer to him. Whatever the present moment may bring, your knowledge that it is his will, and that your future heavenly life will be influenced by it, will make all not only tolerable, but welcome to you, while no vicissitudes can affect you greatly, knowing that he who holds you in his powerful hand cannot change but abideth forever.

John Nicholas Grou
Manual for Interior Souls

It seems to me that real liberty consists in obeying God in all things, and in following the light which points out our duty, and the grace which guides us; taking as our rule of life the intention to please God in all things; not only always to do what is acceptable to him, but if possible what is *most* acceptable; not trifling with petty distinctions between sins great and small, imperfections and faults – for although it may be very true that there are such distinctions, they should have no weight with a soul which is determined to refuse nothing it possesses to God. It is in this sense that the Apostle says, 'The law is not made for a righteous man' – a burdensome, hard, threatening law, one might almost say a tyrannical, enslaving law; but there is a higher law which rises above all this, and leads him into the true 'liberty of sons' – the law which makes him always strive to do that which is most pleasing to his Heavenly Father, in the spirit of those beautiful words of St Augustine: 'Love and do what thou wilt.'

François Fenelon
Letters to Women

Let us live for love, always surrendered, immolating ourselves at every moment, by doing God's will without searching for extraordinary things.

Blessed Elizabeth of the Trinity

To love God's will when all goes well is to love aright, as long as we really do love his will and not the comfortable effects of it. Nevertheless, it is a love that knows no opposition, no reluctance, no effort; surely anyone would love a will so deserving of love, so attractively portrayed. To love God's will in his commandments, counsels, inspirations, is a stage higher, much more perfect. This leads us to give up and forgo our own wills, our own desires, so that we deprive ourselves of pleasure up to a point. To love suffering and distress out of love for God is charity's highest degree. There is nothing, then, to attract us but God's will; it goes very much against the grain of our nature; it leads to more than giving up pleasure – we actually choose toil and trouble.

St Francis of Sales
The Love of God

Let each look to himself and see what God wants of him and attend to this, leaving all else alone.

Henry Suso

You will say to me: how can I glorify him? That is a very simple matter. Our Lord gave us the secret when he told us: 'My meat is to do the will of him who sent me' (John 4:34).

Hold fast therefore to the will of this adorable Master, look on every suffering as well as every joy, as coming directly from him, and then your life will be like a continual communion, for everything will be, as it were, a sacrament which gives you God himself. And that is perfectly true, for God cannot be divided; his will is his entire being. He is totally present in everything and everything is, in a sense, an emanation of his love. You can see therefore how easily you can glorify him in times of suffering and insufferable weariness.

Forget about yourself as far as you can, for that is the secret of peace and happiness. St Francis Xavier used to exclaim: 'What concerns me, does not move; but what concerns him moves me powerfully.' Happy the soul who has arrived at this total detachment; she really loves!

Blessed Elizabeth of the Trinity
Spiritual Writings

This transforming of the will in love, this simplifying and supernaturalizing of the whole drive and intention of our life, by its immersion in the great movement of the Infinite Life, is itself the work of Creative Spirit. It is only possible because that Spirit already indwells the soul's ground, and there pursues the secret alchemy of love, more and more possessing and transmuting us, with every small movement of acceptance or renunciation in which we yield ourselves to the quiet action of God.

Evelyn Underhill
The Golden Sequence

To love God is to will what he wills.

Charles de Foucauld

Divine Providence

One of the great French teachers of the seventeenth century, Cardinal de Bérulle, summed up the relation of man to God in three words: Adoration, Adherence, Co-operation. This means, that from first to last the emphasis is to be on God and not on ourselves. Admiring delight, not cadging demands. Faithful and childlike dependence – a clinging to the Invisible, as the most real of all realities, in all the vicissitudes of life – not mere self-expression and self-fulfilment. Disinterested collaboration in the Whole, in God's vast plan and purpose; not concentration on our own small affairs. Three kinds of generosity. Three kinds of self-forgetfulness. There we have the formula of the spiritual life: a confident reliance on the immense fact of his Presence, everywhere and at all times, pressing on the soul and the world by all sorts of paths and in all sorts of ways, pouring out on it his undivided love, and demanding an undivided loyalty. The discovery that this is happening all the time, to the just and the unjust – and that we are simply being invited to adore and to serve that which is already there – once it has become a living conviction for us, will inevitably give to our spiritual life a special quality of gratitude, realism, trust.

Evelyn Underhill
The Spiritual Life

As verily as we shall be in the bliss of God without end, him praising and thanking, so we have been in the foresight of God, loved and known in his endless purpose from without beginning. In which beginning love he made us; and in the same love he keepeth us and never suffereth us to be hurt (in any way) by which our bliss might be lost. And therefore when the Doom is given and we be all brought up above, then (shall) we clearly see in God the privities which now be hidden to us. Then shall none of us be stirred to say in any wise: 'Lord, if it had been thus, then it had been full well'; but we shall say all with one voice: 'Lord, blessed mayst Thou be, for it is thus: it is well.'

Julian of Norwich
Revelations of Divine Love

God wishes each of us to work as hard as we can, holding nothing back but giving ourselves to the utmost, and when we can do no more, then is the moment when the hand of Divine Providence is stretched out to us and takes over.

Don Orione

Our life is at the mercy of providence, and providence is not a mere course of external events; but the significant will of Three Divine Persons, one God. Our condition in the next life is known to him already; and we on our part know that more grace than he is obliged to give is necessary for us, although we know of an infallible certainty that he will give it us, if we choose to correspond to what we have. Yet this last consideration cannot wholly allay the nervousness which the view of our position naturally causes us. Reflection on the attributes of God, his omniscience, omnipotence, immensity, and ineffable holiness, is not calculated to diminish this feeling. Nevertheless, the conviction that the spirit of adoration, the temper of worship, the instinct of religiousness, reside simply in our always feeling, speaking, and acting towards God as creatures, that is, as beings who have no independent existence but have been called out of nothing by him, is in reality so far from projecting a gloomy shadow over us, or exciting an internal disquietude, that the more seriously these truths are received into the soul, and the more unreservedly the sovereignty of God is acknowledged by us, the more tranquillizing, supernaturally tranquillizing, will their effect be found.

Frederick William Faber
Growth in Holiness

In all created things discern the Providence and wisdom of God, and in all things give him thanks.

St Teresa of Avila

Everything is governed with supreme wisdom by the will of God. The effect which he has ordained that a particular event, a certain grace, should produce in us, depends on a certain exact moment when he sees that our heart will be favourably disposed. Earlier than that moment would be too soon; after it would be too late. What is useful to you today would have been of no use yesterday and will not be tomorrow.

John Nicholas Grou
The School of Jesus Christ

Just walk on uninterruptedly and very quietly; if God makes you run he will enlarge your heart.

St Francis of Sales
Letters

Abandonment to the Will of God

There was a learned man who, eight years long, desired that God would show him a man who would teach him the truth. And once when he felt a very great longing a voice from God came to him and said, 'Go to the church and there shalt thou find a man who shall show thee the way to blessedness.' And he went there, and found a poor man whose feet were torn and covered with dust and dirt: and all his clothes were hardly worth three farthings. And he greeted him saying:

'God give you good day!'
He answered: 'I have never had a bad day!'
'God give you good luck.'
'I have never had ill luck.'
'May you be happy! But why do you answer me thus?'
'I have never been unhappy.'
'Pray explain this to me, for I cannot understand it.'
The poor man answered, 'Willingly. You wished me good

day. I have never had a bad day: for if I am hungry I praise God; if it freezes, hails, snows, rains, if the weather is fair or foul, still I praise God; am I wretched and despised, I praise God, and so I have never had an evil day. You wished that God would send me luck. But I have never had ill luck, for I know how to live with God, and I know that what he does is best; and what God gives me or ordains for me, be it good or ill, I take it cheerfully from God as the best that can be, and so I have never had ill luck. You wished that God would make me happy. I was never unhappy; for my only desire is to live in God's will, and I have so entirely yielded my will to God's, that what God wills, I will.'

'But if God should cast you into hell!' said the learned man. 'What would you do then?'

'Cast me into hell? His goodness forbids! But if he did cast me into hell I should have two arms to embrace him. One arm is true humility, that I should lay beneath him, and be thereby united to his holy humanity. And with the right arm of love, which is united with his holy divinity, I should so embrace him that he would have to go to hell with me. And I would rather be in hell and have God, than in heaven and not have God.'

Then the Master understood that true abandonment with utter humility is the nearest way to God.

Meister Eckhart
From *Mysticism* by
Evelyn Underhill

Give up yourself to God without reserve; in singleness of heart, meeting everything that every day brings forth, as something that comes from God, and is to be received and gone through by you, in such an heavenly use of it, as you would suppose the holy Jesus would have done, in such occurrences. This is an attainable degree of perfection.

William Law
A Call to the Devout Life

Only two things are necessary; firstly, the profound conviction that nothing happens in this world, in our souls or outside them, without the design or permission of God; now, we ought to submit ourselves no less to what God permits than to what he directly wills; secondly, the firm belief that through the all-powerful and paternal Providence of God, all that he wills or permits invariably turns to the advantage of those who practise this submission to his orders. Supported by this double assurance, let us remain firm and unshakeable in our adhesion to all that it may please God to ordain with regard to us, let us acquiesce in advance, in a spirit of humility, love and sacrifice in all imaginable dispositions of his Providence, let us protest that we wish to be content with whatever satisfies him. We shall not always be able, no doubt, to feel this contentment in the lower (the sensitive) part of our soul, but we shall at least preserve it on the heights of our spirit, on the fine point of our will, as St Francis de Sales says, and in those circumstances it will be even more meritorious.

Jean-Pierre de Caussade
Self-Abandonment to
Divine Providence

Now self-abandonment is my only guide, the only compass I have to steer by; there's nothing I can pray for eagerly except the fulfilment of God's will for my soul, unhindered by any intrusion of created things.

St Thérèse of Lisieux
Autobiography of a Saint

'Offer a sacrifice of justice,' says the Prophet, 'and hope in the Lord.' This means that the great and solid foundation of the spiritual life is to give oneself to God in order to be the subject of his good pleasure in everything internal and external, and afterwards to forget oneself so completely that one considers oneself as a thing sold and delivered to the purchaser to which one has no longer any right, in such a way that the good pleasure of God makes all our joy and his happiness, glory and being become our sole good.

This foundation being laid, the soul has nothing to do save to pass all her life in rejoicing that God is good, abandoning herself so completely to his good pleasure that she is equally content to do this or that, or the contrary, at the disposal of God, without reflecting on the use which his good pleasure makes of her.

To abandon oneself! This then is the great duty which remains to be fulfilled after we have acquitted ourselves faithfully of the duties of our state. The perfection with which this duty is accomplished will be the measure of our sanctity.

A holy soul is but a soul freely submitted to the Divine will with the help of grace. All that follows this simple acquiescence is the work of God and not of man. This should blindly resign herself in self-abandonment and universal indifference. This is the only disposition asked of her by

God; the rest belongs to him to choose and determine according to his designs, as an architect selects and marks the stones of the building he proposes to construct.

We should then love God and his order in everything, and we should love it as it presents itself, desiring nothing more. That these or those objects should be presented is no concern of the soul, but of God, and what he gives is best. The whole of spirituality can be expressed in abridged form in this maxim: we should abandon ourselves purely and entirely to the Order of God, and when we are in that Order we should with a complete self-forgetfulness be eternally busied with loving and obeying him, without all these fears, reflections, returns on ourselves, and disquietudes which sometimes result from the care of our own salvation and perfection. Since God offers to manage our affairs for us, let us once and for all hand them over to his infinite wisdom, in order to occupy ourselves only with himself and what belongs to him.

Jean-Pierre de Caussade
*Self-Abandonment to
Divine Providence*

Chapter Nine

Strength in Need

Affliction

When we hit a nail with a hammer, the whole of the shock received by the large head of the nail passes into the point without any of it being lost, although it is only a point. If the hammer and the head of the nail were infinitely big it would be just the same. The point of the nail would transmit this infinite shock at the point to which it was applied.

Extreme affliction, which means physical pain, distress of soul, and social degradation, all at the same time, constitutes the nail. The point is applied at the very centre of the soul. The head of the nail is all the necessity which spreads throughout the totality of space and time.

Affliction is a marvel of divine technique. It is a simple and ingenious device which introduces into the soul of a finite creature the immensity of force, blind, brutal, and cold. The infinite distance which separates God from the creature is entirely concentrated into one point to pierce the soul in its centre . . .

He whose soul remains ever turned in the direction of God while the nail pierces it, finds himself nailed on to the very centre of the universe. It is the true centre, it is not in the middle, it is beyond space and time, it is God. In a dimension which does not belong to space, which is not in time, which is indeed quite a different dimension, this nail has pierced a hole through all creation, through the thickness of the screen which separates the soul from God. In this marvellous dimension the soul, without leaving the place and the instant where the body to which it is united is situated, can cross the totality of space and time and come into the very presence of God.

It is at the intersection of creation and its Creator. This point of intersection is the point of intersection of the branches of the Cross.

Simone Weil
Waiting on God

The chief pang of most trials is not so much the actual suffering itself, as our own spirit of resistance to it.

John Nicholas Grou

He has an especial tenderness of love towards thee for that thou art in the dark and hast no light, and his heart is glad when thou doest arise and say, 'I will go to my Father'. For he sees thee through all the gloom in which thou canst not see him. Say to him, 'My God, I am very dull and low and hard; but thou art wise and high and tender, and thou art my God. I am thy child. Forsake me not.' Then fold the arms of thy faith, and wait in quietness until light goes up in thy darkness. Fold the arms of thy Faith, I say, but not of thy Action: bethink thee of something that thou oughtest to do, and go and do it, if it be but the sweeping of a room, or the preparing of a meal, or a visit to a friend; heed not thy feelings: do thy work.

George MacDonald

Better it is to be heavy-laden and near one that is strong than relieved of one's load and near one that is weak. When thou art heavy-laden, thou art near to God, who is thy strength and is with them that are in trouble. When thou art relieved, thou art near but to thyself, who art thine own weakness. For the virtue and strength of the soul grows and is confirmed by trials of patience.

He that desires to be alone without the support of a master and guide will be like the tree that is alone in the field and has no owner. However much fruit it bears, passers-by will pluck it all, and it will not mature.

The tree that is cultivated and kept with the favour of its owner gives in due season the fruit that is expected of it.

The soul that is alone and without a master, and has virtue, is like the burning coal that is alone. It will grow colder rather than hotter.

He that falls alone remains on the ground alone and holds his soul of small account, since he trusts it to himself alone.

If thou fearest not to fall alone, how dost thou presume to rise alone? See how much more can be done by two together than by one alone!

St John of the Cross
Spiritual Sentences and Maxims

Be patient not only with regard to the essential affliction but also with regard to all those accidental inconveniences that go with it. Many people are quite prepared to be afflicted so long as they are not inconvenienced. 'I would not mind being poor,' says one, 'if only it did not prevent me from helping my friends, bringing up my children properly, and from living as honourably as I should like'; another will say, 'I should not mind being poor if only the wealthy did not think it was through my own fault'; another is quite prepared to bear slander patiently so long as no one believes it; others again are prepared to put up with some of the inconveniences of an evil but not with all of them. They say they are impatient not because they are ill, but because they cannot pay for the proper treatment, or because their illness inconveniences others, but I say that we must bear patiently, not only illness, but the particular illness which God wills, where he wills it, amongst whom he wills it and with all the inconveniences that he wills; and so on with regard to other trials.

When any evil befalls you take the remedies within your power according to God's will; to do otherwise would be tempting God; but having taken such remedies leave the outcome to God's good pleasure with complete resignation. If they are successful, thank him humbly; if not, bless him with patience, which very few people do.

St Francis of Sales
Introduction to the Devout Life

Why make a misery of those troubles which belong to our earthly state and which happen to every one? We may dislike them, but there is nothing to be surprised about in that, and after all there are other much worse evils. A sturdy common sense is always necessary. People generally think less ill of us than we believe. They like us in reality more than they appear to do or than we wish. Instead of 'ill-will' we should say 'lack of goodwill' (through narrowness, stupidity, ignorance or weakness). It is in the midst of all this that we have to live in this world and none of it has ever prevented us from living. It serves us right and though it may not do us any particular good, yet it is not 'death itself' . . .

When God destines us for suffering, it is far better to go

through it, even though we often fail, and meet with spiritual reverses, than not to have had the experience; to remain untouched because we have not suffered. Why? Because the merit of suffering (whose value in the eyes of God, who is so good and tender, is beyond all measure), far exceeds if willed and accepted all that we could lose by any weaknesses which arose from such suffering. It is rather like the merit of those who have gone through the test of life. With all their faults, they rank higher in glory than those perfectly pure children who died directly after baptism. As therefore God has allowed you to suffer, you are more pleasing in his eyes, even though interiorly or exteriorly sinful, than if you were absolutely sinless, thanks to not having had to bear suffering. Praise God! All this is really without the slightest doubt!

Abbé de Tourville
Letters of Direction

He who knoweth how to suffer will enjoy much peace. Such a one is a conqueror of himself and lord of the world, a friend of Christ, and an heir of heaven.

Thomas à Kempis
The Imitation of Christ

In order to give glory to God and overcome suffering with the charity of Christ:

Suffer without reflection, without hate, suffer with no hope of revenge or compensation, suffer without being impatient for the end of suffering.

Neither the beginning of suffering is important nor its ending. Neither the source of suffering is important nor its explanation, provided it be God's will. But we know that he does not will useless, that is to say sinful, suffering. Therefore in order to give him glory we must be quiet and humble and poor in all that we suffer, so as not to add to our sufferings the burden of a useless and exaggerated sensibility.

In order to suffer without dwelling on our own affliction, we must think about a greater affliction, and turn to Christ on the Cross. In order to suffer without hate we must drive out bitterness from our heart by loving Jesus. In order to suffer without hope of compensation, we should find all our peace in the conviction of our union with Jesus. These things are not a matter of ascetic technique but of simple faith: they mean nothing without prayer, without desire, without the acceptance of God's will.

In the end, we must seek more than a passive acceptance of whatever comes to us from him, we must desire and seek in all things the positive fulfilment of his will. We must suffer with gratitude, glad of a chance to do his will. And we must find, in this fulfilment, a communion with Jesus, who said: 'With desire have I desired to eat this Pasch with you before I suffer' (Luke 22:15).

Thomas Merton
No Man is an Island

Encouragement

You perhaps will say that all people fall short of the perfection of the Gospel, and therefore you are content with your failings. But this is saying nothing to the purpose: for the question is not whether Gospel perfection can be fully attained, but whether you come as near it as a sincere intention and careful diligence can carry you. Whether you are not in a much lower state than you might be if you sincerely intended and carefully laboured to advance yourself in all Christian virtues.

William Law
A Serious Call to a
Devout and Holy Life

I know no one so good that he has not need to look ceaselessly into and test and know his heart, what is therein; and also often to find fault with all he does, which must be done with humility. God's voice taught me this because I never did anything so well that I could not have done it better. My weaknesses reproved me thus. 'Ah wretched creature! how long wilt thou hide thy useless habits in thy five senses? Our childhood was foolish, and youth troubled; how we conquered it is known only to God. Alas! now in my old age I find much to chide, for it can produce no shining works and is cold and without grace. It is powerless, now that it no longer has youth to help it to bear the fiery love of God. It is also impatient, for little ills afflict it much which in youth it hardly noticed. Yet a good old age is full of patient waiting and trusts in God alone.'

Seven years ago a troubled old soul lamented these weaknesses to our Lord. God answered thus: 'Thy childhood was a companion to my Holy Spirit; thy youth was a bride of my humanity, in thine old age thou art a humble house-wife of my Godhead.'

Mechthild of Magdeburg
Revelations

Be patient with everyone, but above all with yourself. I mean, do not be disturbed because of your imperfections, and always rise up bravely from a fall. I am glad that you make a daily new beginning; there is no better means of progress in the spiritual life than to be continually beginning afresh, and never to think that we have done enough.

St Francis of Sales

Discouragement is an inclination to give up all attempts after the devout life, in consequence of the difficulties by which it is beset, and our already numerous failures in it. We lose heart; and partly in ill-temper, partly in real doubt of our own ability to persevere, we first grow querulous and peevish with God, and then relax in our efforts to mortify ourselves and to please him. It is a sort of shadow of despair, and will lead us into numberless venial sins the first half-hour we give way to it.

Frederick William Faber

Every morning compose your soul for a tranquil day, and all through it be careful often to recall your resolution, and bring yourself back to it, so to say. If something discomposes you, do not be upset, or troubled; but having discovered the fact, humble yourself gently before God, and try to bring your mind into a quiet attitude. Say to yourself, 'Well, I have made a false step; now I must go more carefully and watchfully.' Do this each time, however frequently you fall. When you are at peace use it profitably, making constant acts of meekness, and seeking to be calm even in the most trifling

155

things. Above all, do not be discouraged; be patient; wait; strive to attain a calm, gentle spirit.

St Francis of Sales
Introduction to a Devout Life

Should we feel at times disheartened and discouraged, a confiding thought, a simple movement of heart towards God will renew our powers. Whatever he may demand of us, he will give us at the moment the strength and the courage that we need.

François Fenelon

The Sacraments, Baptism and Eucharist

Sanctity may be defined as: 'a divine life, communicated and received.' This life is communicated from above, by God, by Christ. It is received by man, from the moment of his baptism. This sacrament confers the grace of adoption and thus sanctifies the soul; it brings to it, as it were, the dawn of the divine life, but this brightness is intended to increase steadily to the glory of a noon that will not fade. Baptismal or sanctifying grace implants in the soul a capacity to share in the very nature of God, by knowledge, by love, and by the possession of the divinity in an intuitive manner which is natural to God alone. This divine gift establishes in man a wonderful and supernatural participation in the divine life.

Columba Marmion
Christ the Ideal of the Priest

Our adoptive sonship is in its supernatural reality a reflection of the sonship of the Word. God has not communicated to us the whole of his nature but a participation of it.

R. Garrigou-Lagrange

May not God say to us what he once said by the voice of his prophet: 'I passed by thee and saw thee: and behold thy time was the time of lovers, and I spread my garment over thee and I entered into a covenant with thee and thou became mine' (Ezekiel 16:8). Yes, we have become his by Baptism, which is what St Paul means by the words: 'He has called them', called them to receive the seal of the Blessed Trinity. By Baptism we were made, in St Peter's words (2 Peter 1:4), 'partakers of the divine nature' and received 'the principle by which we are grounded in him'. Then 'he justified us', by his sacraments, by his direct touches when we were recollected in the depths of our soul. He has also justified us by faith and according to the measure of our faith in the redemption acquired for us by Jesus Christ. Lastly he wills 'to glorify us', and therefore, says St Paul, he has 'made us fit to share the light which saints inherit' (Colossians 1:12). But we shall be glorified in the measure in which we have been 'moulded into the image of his son'.

Blessed Elizabeth of the Trinity
Spiritual Writings

It is above all by Sacramental Communion that we now assimilate the fruits of this dying and rising of Christ.

What, indeed, do we receive in the Eucharist? We receive Christ, the Body and Blood of Christ. But if Communion supposes the immolation of Calvary and that of the Altar which reproduces it, it is however the glorified Flesh of the Saviour wherewith we communicate. We receive Christ such as he is now, that is to say glorified in the highest heavens and possessing, in its fullest expansion, the glory of his Resurrection.

He whom we thus really receive is the very Fount of holiness. He cannot fail to give us a share in the grace of his 'holy' Resurrection; here, as in all things, it is of his fullness that we are all to receive.

Still in our days, Christ, ever living, repeats to each soul the words that he said to his disciples when at the time of the Pasch, he was about to institute his Sacrament of love. 'With desire, I have desired to eat *this pasch* with you' (Luke 22:15). Christ Jesus desires to effect in us the mystery of his Resurrection: He lives entirely for his Father above all that is earthly; he wills, for our joy, to draw us with him into this divine current. If, after having received him in Communion, we leave him full power to act, he will give to our life, by the inspirations of his Spirit, that steadfast orientation towards the Father in which all holiness is summed up; so all our thoughts, all our aspirations, all our activity will refer to the glory of our Father in heaven.

Columba Marmion
Christ in His Mysteries

What impresses me is that this centre of the Eucharist is hidden, invisible, altogether interior and, for all that, most real, living and sustaining.

Jesus draws the soul spiritually into the wholly spiritualized state that is his in the sacrament.

What, in fact, is the nature of the life of Jesus in the most Blessed Sacrament? It is entirely hidden, all interior.

158

He conceals therein his power and kindness; he conceals his divine person. And all his actions and virtues take on this simple and hidden character.

He requires silence around him. He no longer prays to his Father 'with a strong cry and tears' as in the Garden of Olives, but through his self-abasement.

Such must the kingdom of Jesus be in me, all interior. I must gather myself up around Jesus: my faculties, my understanding, and my will, and my senses, as far as possible. I must live of Jesus and not of myself, in Jesus and not in myself. I must pray with him, immolate myself with him, and be consumed in the same love with him. I must become in him one flame, one heart, one life with him.

What nourishes this centre is something similar to God's call to Abraham, *egredere* – go forth out of thy country. It is the renouncing and abandoning of outside things; the turning to those within and the losing of oneself in Jesus. This manner of life is more pleasing to his heart and gives greater glory to his Father. That is why our Lord desires it ardently. He tells us: 'Come out of thyself and follow me into solitude where, alone with thee, I will speak to thy heart.'

This life of Jesus is nothing other than the love of predilection, the gift of self, the intensifying of union with him. Through it we take root, as it were, and prepare the nourishment, the sap of the tree. *Regnum Dei intra vos est.* 'The kingdom of God is within you.'

Peter Julian Eymard

Thanksgiving

Would you know who is the greatest saint in the world? It is not he who prays most or fasts most; it is not he who gives

159

most alms, but it is he who is always thankful to God, who receives everything as an instance of God's goodness and has a heart always ready to praise God for it.

If anyone would tell you the shortest, surest way to all happiness and perfection, he must tell you to make a rule to thank and praise God for everything that happens to you. Whatever seeming calamity happens to you, if you thank and praise God for it, you turn it into a blessing. Could you therefore work miracles you could not do more for yourself than by this thankful spirit; it turns all that it touches into happiness.

William Law
A Serious Call to a
Devout and Holy Life

One act of thanksgiving when things go wrong with us is worth a thousand thanks when things are agreeable to our inclination.

Blessed John of Avila

Noble souls feel the need to testify to their gratitude; there are other souls who can only think of themselves; they feel that they are entitled to everything and do not give thanks for anything. A character which is both great and humble may almost be said to suffer from this constant desire to express its gratitude. Consider St Teresa: she had a heart as wide as the sands of the sea-shore, she experienced this thirst for thanksgiving; her heart was on the point of breaking under the strain of this torment. The writings of St Gertrude also express this same greatness of soul. In her transport of gratitude, she liked to recall to the Holy Trinity all the favours which had been lavished on her from her childhood. The whole of her magnificent book of exercises, *The Herald of Divine Love*, is simply a canticle of grateful praise.

In this these great saints were only imitating their divine Spouse. The heart of Christ was the most noble that has ever existed. During the course of his mortal life he thanked the Father and even now he still offers him thanks. He gives thanks first of all on his own behalf because his humanity has been assumed by the divine Person of the Word: because it belongs to the Word and shares his glory. On account of this grace of the hypostatic union it owes more to God than the whole of the human race.

Jesus thanked the Father also on our behalf in his capacity as Chief and Saviour: 'He rejoiced in the Holy Ghost,' St Luke tells us, 'and said, "I confess to Thee, O Father, Lord of heaven and earth, because Thou hast hidden these things from the wise and prudent and hast revealed them to little ones. Yes, Father, for so it hath seemed good in Thy sight" ' (Luke 10:21–22).

Columba Marmion
Christ the Ideal of the Priest

Thou hast given so much to me
Give one thing more – a grateful heart:
Not thankful when it pleaseth me,
As if thy blessings had spare days,
But such a heart whose Pulse may be
Thy Praise.

George Herbert
A Heart to Praise Thee

Chapter Ten

Union With God

Contemplation

What is more easy and sweet than meditation? Yet in this hath God commended his love, that by meditation it is enjoyed. As nothing is more easy than to think, so nothing is more difficult than to think well. The easiness of thinking we receive from God, the difficulty of thinking well proceeded from ourselves. Yet in truth, it is far more easy to think well than ill, because good thoughts be sweet and delightful: evil thoughts are full of discontent and trouble. So that an evil habit and custom have made it difficult to think well, not nature. For by nature nothing is so difficult as to think amiss.

Is it not easy to conceive the world in your mind? To think the heavens fair? The sun glorious? The earth fruitful? The air pleasant? The sea profitable? And the giver bountiful? Yet these are the things which it is difficult to retain. For could we always be sensible of their use and value, we should be always delighted with their wealth and glory.

Thomas Traherne
Centuries of Meditations

It is clear that those who have progressed a certain distance in the interior life not only do not need to make systematic meditations, but rather profit by abandoning them in favour of a simple and peaceful affective prayer, without fuss, without voice, without much speech, and with no more than one or two favourite ideas or mysteries, to which they return in a more or less general and indistinct manner each time they pray.

Thomas Merton
What Are These Wounds?

Every Christian is called already here on earth to a minimum of loving knowledge of God, in the light of the gifts of the Holy Spirit, and without it he would be incapable of praying, of loving God and of living according to the Gospel. This fundamental unity of the Christian life, which underlies the variety of tasks and charismas, has been freshly appreciated in recent times. All possess the same life with its essential elements even though all are not called to develop them in the same way. This union of knowledge and love that we have named contemplation, acquired or given charismatically, thus appears to us as necessarily one of these elements essential to all Christian life. If contemplation must exist in every Christian at least as a seed, it is desirable that this seed develop as much as possible, to the very measure of generosity and charity. This seed cannot wither in the heart of a Christian without serious damage to the integrity and perfection of his Christian life.

René Voillaume
*Contemplation in the Church
of Our Time*

He who keeps his heart within, he it is who receives the light of contemplation. For they that still think immoderately of external things know not what are the chinks of contemplation from the eternal light. For that infusion of incorporeal light is not received along with the images of corporeal things because while only visible things are thought of, the invisible light is not admitted to the mind.

St Gregory the Great
Homily on Ezekiel

Contemplation is the fullness of the Christian vocation, the full flowering of baptismal grace of the Christ-life in our souls.

Thomas Merton

What is this dryness in meditation which I am describing; this refusal to fix our thoughts on spiritual things? Clearly it may depend on some fault in ourselves. It may depend on some unhealthy attachment in our hearts, lack of vigilance, or the thorns in which we have let the good seed be choked. Difficulty in meditation is not always the sign of an advance of the soul towards God, or the progress to a higher type of prayer.

But it may, thank God, be a sign of that. How can one know the difference?

Again John of the Cross tells us.

There are three signs which indicate the movement from discursive to contemplative prayer:

1. We lack the desire to use the imagination.

2. The imagination and the senses no longer have the will to think about specific things. The things of the earth offer no consolation.

3. The soul wants to remain still, directed towards God

164

alone. It desires inner peace, quiet and repose; it no longer feels the need to use the human faculties.

This third condition is good. If it is present in the soul it justifies the other two. If I have difficulty in meditating on God, if I no longer succeed in fixing my attention on one mystery or another in the life of Jesus, on one truth or another, but I am craving to remain alone and motionless and silent at the feet of God, empty of thought but in an act of love . . . it means something great. It is one of the most beautiful secrets of the spiritual life.

Carlo Carretto
Letters from the Desert

How the work of contemplation shall be done
This is what you are to do: lift your heart up to the Lord, with a gentle stirring of love desiring him for his own sake and not for his gifts. Centre all your attention and desire on him and let this be the sole concern of your mind and heart. Do all in your power to forget everything else, keeping your thoughts and desires free from involvement with any of God's creatures or their affairs whether in general or in particular. Perhaps this will seem like an irresponsible attitude, but I tell you, let them all be; pay no attention to them.

What I am describing here is the contemplative work of the spirit. It is this which gives God the greatest delight. For when you fix your love on him, forgetting all else, the saints and angels rejoice and hasten to assist you in every way — though the devils will rage and ceaselessly conspire to thwart you. Your fellowmen are marvellously enriched by this work of yours, even if you may not fully understand how; the souls in purgatory are touched, for their suffering is eased by the effects of this work; and, of course, your own spirit is purified and strengthened by this contemplative work more than by all others put together. Yet for all this, when God's grace arouses you to enthusiasm, it becomes the lightest sort of work there is and one most willingly done. Without his grace, however, it is very difficult and almost, I should say, quite beyond you.

And so diligently persevere until you feel joy in it. For in the beginning it is usual to feel nothing but a kind of darkness about your mind, or as it were, a *cloud of unknowing*. You will seem to know nothing and to feel nothing except a naked intent toward God in the depths of your being. Try as you might, this darkness and this cloud will remain between you and your God. You will feel frustrated, for your mind will be unable to grasp him, and your heart will not relish the delight of his love. But learn to be at home in this darkness. Return to it as often as you can, letting your spirit cry out to him whom you love. For if, in this life, you hope to feel and see God as he is in himself it must be within this darkness and this cloud. But if you strive to fix your love on him forgetting all else, which is the work of contemplation I have urged you to begin, I am confident that God in his goodness will bring you to a deep experience of himself.

The Anonymous Author of
The Cloud of Unknowing

Contemplation is nothing else but an experience of God revealing himself to us in the intimate embrace of a love so pure that it overwhelms every other affection and excludes everything from our souls but the knowledge of love alone.

Thomas Merton
New Seeds of Contemplation

Contemplation and Action

The contemplation of Christ, the friend of men, must give us the habit of looking at them as Jesus himself looked at them – from the perspective of their eternity. So expanded a look of love penetrates to that emptiness there is in every man, which only God can fill. There is a way of loving men which opens their eyes to their own mystery. To know and love men from within such a vision, far from turning contemplation away from God, leads one back to him constantly. It is then that friendship for men nourishes, so to speak, the fire of contemplation, of which love is the measure; but this of course is on condition that we know how to keep away from the illusions and mirages of a friendship folded in on itself or limited by earthly horizons.

René Voillaume
Contemplation in the Church
of Our Time

Action and contemplation now grow together into one life and one unity. They become two aspects of the same thing. Action is charity looking outward to others men, and contemplation is charity drawn inward to its own divine source. Action is the stream, and contemplation is the spring. The spring remains more important than the stream, for the only thing that really matters is for love to spring up inexhaustibly from the infinite abyss of Christ and God.

Thomas Merton
No Man is an Island

None is permitted to lead a life of pure contemplation in such a way that in his leisure he would not mind his neighbour's needs. On the other hand, no man should be busy in such a manner as to have no desire to contemplate God. His leisure should not be a rest without action, but either searching or finding of truth, and this in a way which would profit his neighbour through our own growth and personal stability.

There are two lives represented in Christ's body: one temporal, in which we labour; the other eternal, in which we contemplate God's delight. The first Christ represented to us in his passion, the other in his resurrection.

Two persons were in the house at Bethany, both blameless, both praiseworthy, two ways of life and with them the source of life: Martha, an image of the present life; and Mary, signifying the future life. Both were friends of the Lord, both lovable, both his disciples. What Martha did, we are. What Mary did, we are in hope of. Let us do one well, so that we obtain the fullness of the other.

St Augustine of Hippo
City of God

The Church is in the world to save the world. It is a tool of God for that purpose; not a comfortable religious club established in fine historical premises. Every one of its members is required, in one way or another, to co-operate with the Spirit in working for that great end: and much of this work will be done in secret and invisible ways. We are transmitters as well as receivers. Our contemplation and our action, our humble self-opening to God, keeping ourselves sensitive to his music and light, and our generous self-opening to our fellow creatures, keeping ourselves sensitive to their needs, ought to form one life; mediating between

God and his world, and bringing the saving power of the Eternal into time. We are far from realizing all that human spirits can do for one another on spiritual levels if they will pay the price; how truly and really our souls interpenetrate, and how impossible and un-Christian it is to 'keep ourselves to ourselves'.

Evelyn Underhill
The Spiritual Life

We are the agents of the Creative Spirit in this world. Real advance in the spiritual life, then, means accepting this vocation with all it involves. Not merely turning over the pages of an engineering magazine and enjoying the pictures, but putting on overalls and getting on with the job. The real spiritual life must be horizontal as well as vertical; spread more and more as well as aspire more and more. It must be larger, fuller, richer, more generous in its interest than the natural life alone can ever be; must invade and transform all homely activities and practical things. For it means an offering of life to the Father of life, to whom it belongs; a willingness – an eager willingness – to take our small place in the vast operations of his Spirit, instead of trying to run a poky little business on our own.

So now we come back to this ordinary mixed life of every day, in which we find ourselves – the life of house and work, tube and tram, newspaper and cinema, with its tangle of problems and suggestions and demands – and consider what we are to do about that; how, within its homely limitations, we can co-operate with the Will. It is far easier, though not very easy, to develop and preserve a spiritual outlook on life, than it is to make our everyday actions harmonize with that spiritual outlook. That means trying to see things, persons and choices from the angle of eternity; and dealing with them as part of the material in which the Spirit works. This will be decisive for the way we behave as to our personal, social, and national obligations. It will decide the papers we read, the movements we support, the kind of administrators we vote for, our attitude to social and international justice. For though we may renounce the world for ourselves, refuse the attempt to get anything out of it, we have to accept it as the sphere in which we are to co-operate with the Spirit, and try to do the Will. Therefore the prevalent notion that spirituality and politics have nothing to do with one another is the exact opposite of the truth. Once it is accepted in a realistic sense, the Spiritual Life has everything to do with politics. It means that certain convictions about God and the world become the moral and spiritual imperatives of our life; and this must be decisive for the way we choose to behave about that bit of the world over which we have been given a limited control.

Evelyn Underhill
The Spiritual Life

When Christ said: 'I was hungry and you fed me', he didn't mean only the hunger for bread and for food; he also meant the hunger to be loved. Jesus himself experienced this loneliness. He came amongst his own and his own received him not, and it hurt him then and it has kept on hurting him. The same hunger, the same loneliness, the same having no one to be accepted by and to be loved and wanted by. Every human being in that case resembles Christ in his loneliness; and that is the hardest part, that's real hunger . . .

Love to pray – feel often during the day the need for prayer, and take trouble to pray. Prayer enlarges the heart until it is capable of containing God's gift of himself. Ask and seek, and your heart will grow big enough to receive him and keep him as your own.

It is not possible to engage in the direct apostolate without being a soul of prayer. We must be aware of oneness with Christ, as he was aware of oneness with his Father. Our activity is truly apostolic only in so far as we permit him to work in us and through us, with his power, with his desire, with his love . . .

Mother Teresa of Calcutta

Darkness Within

The behaviour of beginners of the way of God is not noble, and very much according to their own liking and self-love. Meanwhile God seeks to raise them higher, to draw them out of this miserable manner of loving to a higher state of the love of God, to deliver them from the low usage of the senses and meditation whereby they seek after God in ways so miserable and unworthy of him. He seeks to place them in the way of the spirit wherein they may be more abundantly, and more free from imperfections, commune with God now that they have been for some time tried in the way of goodness, persevering in meditation and prayer, and because of the sweetness they have formed therein have withdrawn their affections from the things of this world, and gained a certain spiritual strength in God, whereby they in some measure curb their love of the creature, and are able, for the love of God, to carry a slight burden of dryness, without going back to that more pleasant time when their spiritual exercises abounded in delights, and when the sun of the divine graces shone, as they think, more clearly upon them. God is now changing that light into darkness, and sealing up the door of the fountain of the sweet spiritual waters, which they tasted in God as often and as long as they wished. For when they were weak and tender, this door was then not shut, as it is written, 'Behold, I have given before thee an opened door, which no man can shut; because thou hast a little strength, and hast kept my word, and hast not denied my name.'

God thus leaves them in darkness so great that they know not whither to betake themselves with their imaginations and reflections of sense. They cannot advance a single step in meditation, as before, the inward sense now being overwhelmed in this night, and abandoned to dryness so great that they have no more any joy or sweetness in their spiritual exercises, as they had before: and in their place they find nothing but insipidity and bitterness. For God now looking upon them as somewhat grown in grace, weans them from the breast that they may become strong, and cast their swaddling clothes aside: he carries them in his arms no longer, and shows them how to walk alone. All this is strange to them, for all things seem to go against them.

St John of the Cross
Dark Night of the Soul

Delivered from the world of sense and the world of thought, the soul enters into the *mysterious darkness of a holy ignorance*, and dismissing all scientific knowledge, it loses itself in him who can neither be seen nor apprehended; it gives itself over completely to this Sovereign Object and belongs no longer to itself or to any other; it is united to the

Unknown by the noblest part of its being in virtue of its renouncement of knowledge; finally, it draws forth from this utter ignorance a knowledge that the intellect would not be able to attain.

Pseudo-Dionysius
Mystical Theology

We are always wanting this and that, and although we have our sweet Jesus resting on our heart we are not satisfied; and yet this is all we can possibly need and desire. One thing alone is necessary – to be near him. You know that at the birth of our Lord the shepherds heard the divine songs of heavenly beings; this is what scripture tells us. But nowhere does it say that Our Lady and Saint Joseph, who were closest to the child, heard the angels' voices or saw the marvellous radiance; on the contrary, they heard the child crying, and by the wretched light of some poor lantern they saw the eyes of this divine boy full of tears and saw him chilled by the cold. Now tell me, would you not rather have been in the dark stable which was full of the baby's crying, rather than with the shepherds ravished with heavenly music and the beauty of this marvellous light?

As St Peter says, it is good for us to be here . . . Love God crucified in the darkness, stay near him and say, 'It is good for me to be here.'

St Francis of Sales
Letter to St Jane de Chantal

I thank you that you, even when I was sitting in darkness, revealed yourself to me, you enlightened me,

you granted me to see the light of your countenance that is
unbearable to all.
I remained seated in the middle of the darkness, I know,
but, while I was there, surrounded by darkness,
you appeared as light, illuminating me completely from
your total light.

And I became light in the night,
I who was found in the midst of darkness.
Neither the darkness extinguished your light completely,
nor did the light dissipate the visible darkness,
but they were together, yet completely separate,
without confusion, far from each other,
surely not at all mixed,
except in the same spot where they filled everything . . .
So I am in the darkness.
yet still I am in the middle of the light.
How can darkness receive within itself a light
and, without being dissipated by the light,
it still remains in the middle of the light?
O awesome wonder which I see doubly,
with my two sets of eyes, of the body and of the soul!
Listen now; I am telling you the awesome mysteries
of a double God who came to me as to a double man.
He took upon himself my flesh and he gave me his Spirit,
and I became also god by divine grace,
a son of God but by adoption.
O what dignity, what glory!

St Symeon the New Theologian
Hymns of Divine Love

Union with God

I confess, though I say it in my foolishness, that the Word has visited me, and even very often. But although he has frequently entered my soul, I have never at any time been sensible of the precise moment of his coming. I have felt that he was present. I remember that he has been with me; I have sometimes been able even to have a presentiment that he would come, but never to feel his coming, nor his departure . . . You will ask then, how, since the ways of his access are thus incapable of being traced, I could know that he was present. But he is living and full of energy, and as soon as he has entered into me he has quickened my sleeping soul; has aroused and softened and goaded my heart, which was in a state of torpor and hard as a stone. He has begun to pluck and destroy, to plant and to build, to water the dry places, to illuminate the gloomy spots, to throw open those which were shut close, to inflame with warmth those which were cold, as also to straighten its crooked paths and make its rough places smooth, so that my soul might bless the Lord, and all that is within me praise his Holy Name. Thus, then, the Bridegroom-Word, though he has several times entered into me, has never made his coming apparent to my sight, hearing or touch. It was not by his motions that he was recognized by me, nor could I tell by any of my senses that he had penetrated to the depths of my being. It was, as I have already said, only by the *movement of my heart* that I was enabled to recognize his presence; and to know the power of his sacred presence by the sudden departure of vices and the strong restraint put upon all carnal affections. From the discovery and conviction of my secret faults I have had good reason to admire the depth of his wisdom; his goodness and kindness have become known in the amendment, whatever it

175

may amount to, of my life; while in the reformation and renewal of the spirit of my mind, that is of my inward man, I have perceived, in a certain degree, the loveliness of his beauty.

St Bernard of Clairvaux
Sermon 74 from *Sermons on
the Song of Songs*

When we are united to Jesus we are *in sinu Patris*. This is the life of *pure love* which presupposes the effort to do always what is most agreeable to the Father.

Columba Marmion

Not content with having adopted me as his child, God has gone further and given me his own Son. God as he is, could he have given me a greater gift, or have given me greater proof of his love? *He that spared not even his own son*, says St Paul, *but delivered him up for us all, how hath he not also, with him, given us all things?* (Romans 8:32). Were I free to ask God for a proof of his love, would such an idea have occurred to me? And if it had, would I have dared to suggest it? There is no need to press the point, for reason itself refuses to entertain such a thought and would refuse to give it credence if faith did not come to its support. Mere human language is not rich enough to express the heart's feelings at the thought of such a grace, and all that we can do is to prostrate ourselves before such a God and beg him to take to himself the glory for his own ineffable gift. To admit that we are absolutely powerless to give him here below the love and thanks he deserves is the only way in which we can acquit ourselves of our debt. We are bound to give him, as our

Father, our all, indeed ourselves, in gratitude for his having given us his Son; but what is the gift of the little we have, of even ourselves; how is the most generous love of which a creature is capable, as a thanksgiving, in any way worthy of this supreme token of God's love for us? On so many counts I already owe him the gift of myself; what have I left to offer him in gratitude for this gift, which is greater than all his other gifts put together?

John Nicholas Grou
Meditations on the Love of God

Only give thyself utterly to Christ – this is the greatest and the most important thing. Place all at his disposal. If thou possess him, he will surely teach thee what thou shouldest do and what thou shouldest give up. He will teach thee to speak for him; he will give the courage and wisdom as to how thou shouldest behave. Be not anxious as to thy dealings with others, but commit it all to him. He will assuredly work within thee that which is well-pleasing in his sight.

Jacob Behmen
Thoughts on the Spiritual Life

We possess God, not in the sense that we become exactly as he, but in that we approach him as closely as possible in a miraculous, spiritual manner, and that our innermost being is illumined and seized by his truth and his holiness.

St Augustine of Hippo

'Live on in me' (John 15:4). It is the Word of God who gives us this command, who expresses this wish. 'Live on in me!', pray in me, adore in me, love in me, suffer in me, work, act in me 'Live on in me', whoever or whatever comes your way, penetrate ever deeper into the dwelling place which is the true 'wilderness where God speaks to the heart', as the Prophet sang. But to understand this wholly mysterious command, we must not remain, so to speak, on the surface; we must enter ever more deeply into the divine Being, by means of recollection. 'I press on' (Philippians 3:12), cried St Paul, and we too should press on every day down the path into the abyss which is God. Let us slip down this steep incline with a confidence rooted in love. 'One depth makes answer to another' (Psalm 42:3–7). There, in the deepest depths, we shall encounter the divine; there the abyss of our nothingness and misery will find itself face to face with the abyss of the mercy of God and with the immensity of the all of God; there we shall find the strength to die to self and, all selfishness purged away, be transformed by love. 'Blessed are those who die in the Lord' (Revelation 14:13).

Blessed Elizabeth of the Trinity
Spiritual Writings

We are the members of Christ, and Christ is our member. And my hand, the hand of one who is the poorest of the poor, is Christ, and my foot is Christ. And I, the poorest of the poor, am the hand of Christ and the foot of Christ. I move my hand, and Christ moves, who is my hand. For you must know that divinity is undivided. I move my foot and my foot shines as he shines. Do not say that this is blasphemy, but confirm this, and adore Christ who has made you in this way. For you also, if such is your desire, will become one of his members. And so all the members of each one of us will become the members of Christ, and Christ our member, and he will make all that is ugly and ill-shapen, beautiful and well-shapen, in that he adores it with the splendour and majesty of his Godhood. And we shall all become gods and intimately united with God, and our bodies will seem to us immaculate, and since we have partaken of the semblance of the whole body of Christ, each one of us shall possess all of Christ. For the one who has become many remains the one undivided, but each part is all of Christ.

Although the many cannot grasp you, verily, in some way you become small within my hands, and you lean down to my lips giving forth light like a shining udder and a sweetness of what is secret. And now give yourself to me that I may allay my hunger with you, that I kiss and clasp your unutterable glory, the light of your countenance, that I be filled, and may communicate to all others, and, when I have departed this life, I may enter into you in glory. May I become light of your light, and stand beside you and be free from care and affliction; liberate me also from the fear that I may not return to you. Give me this also, Lord, grant me this also, since you have given me, who am unworthy, all else. For this is the most needful, and in this is all.

Symeon the Younger
Quoted in *The Spear of God*

Life in the Trinity

I beheld the working of the blessed Trinity: in which beholding I saw and understood these three properties: the property of the Fatherhood, the property of the Motherhood, and the property of the Lordhood, in one God. In our Father Almighty we have our keeping and our bliss concerning our natural substance, which is ours by our making, without beginning. And in the second Person in wit and wisdom we have our keeping concerning our sense soul: our restoring and our saving; for he is our Mother, Brother and Saviour. And in our good Lord the Holy Ghost, we have our rewarding, our portion and our travail, and endless our passing of all that we desire, in his marvellous courtesy, of his high plenteous grace. For all our life is in three: in the first we have our being, in the second we have our increasing, and in the third we have our fulfilling; the first is Nature, the second is Mercy, and the third is Grace. The high might of the Trinity is our Father, and the deep wisdom of the Trinity is our Mother, and the great love of the Trinity is our Lord: and all this we have in Nature and in our substantial making.

Julian of Norwich
Revelations of Divine Love

Thou, O eternal Trinity, art a deep sea, into which the deeper I enter the more I find, and the more I find the more I seek; the soul cannot be satiated in thy abyss, for she continually hungers after thee, the eternal Trinity, desiring to see thee with the light of thy light. As the hart desires the springs of living water, so my soul desires to leave the prison of this dark body and see thee in truth.

St Catherine of Siena

We know well that the bosom of the Father is our ground and origin, in which we begin our being and our life. And from our proper ground, that is from the Father and from all that lives in him, there shines forth an eternal brightness, which is the birth of the Son. And in this brightness, that is, in the Son, the Father knows himself and all that lives in him; for all that he has, and all that he is, he gives to the Son, save only the property of Fatherhood, which abides in himself. And this is why all that lives in the Father, unmanifested in the Unity, is also in the Son actively poured forth into manifestation: and the simple ground of our Eternal Image ever remains in darkness and in waylessness, but the brightness without limit which streams forth from it, this reveals and brings forth within the Conditioned the hiddenness of God. And all those men who are raised up above their created being into a God-seeing life are one with this Divine brightness. And they are that brightness itself, and they see, feel, and find, even by means of this Divine Light, that, as regards their uncreated essence, they are that same onefold ground from which the brightness without limit shines forth in the Divine way, and which, according to the simplicity of the Essence, abides eternally onefold and wayless within. And this is why inward and God-seeing men will go out in the way of contemplation, above reason and above distinction and above their created being, through an eternal intuitive gazing. By means of this inborn light they are transfigured, and made one with that same light through which they see and which they see. And thus the God-seeing men follow after their Eternal Image, after which they have been made; and they behold God and all things, without distinction, in a simple seeing, in the Divine brightness. And this is the most noble and the most profitable contemplation to which one can attain in this life; for in this contemplation, a man best remains master of himself and free. And at each loving introversion he may grow in nobility of life beyond anything that we are able to understand; for he remains free and master of himself in inwardness and virtue. And this gazing at the Divine Light holds him up above all inwardness and all virtue and all merit, for it is the crown and the reward after which we strive, and which we have and possess now in this wise; for a God-seeing life is a heavenly life. But were we set free from this misery and this exile, so we should have, as regards our created being, a greater capacity to receive this brightness; and so the glory of God would shine through us in every way better and more nobly. This is the way above all ways, in which one goes out through Divine contemplation and an eternal intuitive gazing, and in which one is transfigured and transmuted in the Divine brightness. This going out of the God-seeing man is also in love; for through the fruition of love he rises above his created being, and finds and tastes the riches and the delights which are God himself, and which he causes to pour forth without interruption in the hiddenness of the spirit, where the spirit is like unto the nobility of God.

When the inward and God-seeing man has thus attained to his Eternal Image, and in this clearness, through the Son, has entered into the bosom of the Father: then he is enlightened by Divine truth, and he receives anew, every moment, the Eternal Birth, and he goes forth according to the way of the light, in a Divine contemplation.

You should know that the heavenly Father, as a living ground, with all that lives in Him, is actively turned towards his Son, as to his own Eternal Wisdom. And that same Wisdom, with all that lives in it, is actively turned back toward the Father, that is, towards that very ground from which it comes forth. And in this meeting, there comes forth the third Person, between the Father and the Son; that is the Holy Ghost, their mutual love, who is one with them both in the same nature. And he enfolds and drenches through both in action and fruition the Father and the Son, and all that lives in both, with such great riches and such joy that as to this all creatures must eternally be silent; for the incomprehensible wonder of this love eternally transcends the understanding of all creatures. But where this wonder is understood and tasted without amazement, there the spirit dwells above itself, and is one with the Spirit of God; and tastes and sees without measure, even as God, the riches which are the spirit itself in the unity of the living ground, where it possesses itself according to the way of its uncreated essence.

·Now this rapturous meeting is incessantly and actively renewed in us, according to the way of God; for the Father gives himself in the Son, and the Son gives himself in the Father, in an eternal content and a loving embrace; and this renews itself every moment within the bonds of love. For like as the Father incessantly beholds all things in the birth of his Son, so all things are loved anew by the Father and the Son in the outpouring of the Holy Ghost. And this is the active meeting of the Father and of the Son, in which we are lovingly embraced by the Holy Ghost in eternal love.

Jan van Ruysbroeck
The Adornment of the
Spiritual Marriage

'Our God', wrote St Paul, 'is a consuming fire' (Hebrews 12:29), that is to say, a fire of love, destroying, transforming into itself all that it touches.

For souls given up to its action in the depths of their being, the mystic death, of which St Paul spoke, becomes very simple and easy. They think much less of the work of destruction and detachment, which remains for them to do, than of plunging into the furnace of love burning within them which is the Holy Spirit himself, the same love which, in the blessed Trinity, is the bond between the Father and his Word. They enter into him by living faith and there, in simplicity and peace, they are carried up by him above all things, above all mere feelings into the 'sacred darkness', and transformed into the divine image. In the words of St John, they live 'in fellowship' with the Three Divine Persons. They share their life; and that is the contemplative life.

Blessed Elizabeth of the Trinity
Spiritual Writings

Index of Authors

Numerical reference to the pages where the excerpts can be found

Acknowledgements

The compiler and publishers would like to thank the following for their permission to reproduce material of which they are the publishers or copyright holders. While every effort has been made to trace copyright holders this has not been possible in a few cases. We apologize for any infringement of copyright or failure correctly to acknowledge original sources, and shall be glad to make any necessary corrections at the earliest opportunity.

Burns & Oates Ltd for extracts from *No Man is an Island* by Thomas Merton; extracts from *Meditations on the Love of God* by John Nicholas Grou, in the Orchard Book series. From the same series, extracts from *An Introduction to the Devout Life* and *The Love of God*, both by St Francis of Sales; *Self-Abandonment to Divine Providence* by Jean-Pierre de Caussade SJ. Extracts from the one-volume edition of *The Complete Works of St John of the Cross*, translated by E. Allison Peers.

Geoffrey Chapman, a division of Cassell Ltd, for extracts from *The Spiritual Writings of Blessed Elizabeth of the Trinity*.

The Community of Stanbrook Abbey for extracts of their translation of St Teresa's *The Interior Castle*.

Harper and Row of New York for extracts from *The Way of Christ* by Jacob Boehme.

Penguin Books Ltd for extracts from *Revelations of Divine Love* by Julian of Norwich, translated by Clifton Wolters (Penguin Classics, 1966) copyright © Clifton Wolters, 1966.

The Prior of St Hugh's Charterhouse, Parkminster, Sussex for extracts from *They Speak by Silences* by a Carthusian and translated from the French by a monk of the Charterhouse.

Collins Publishers, for extracts from *Waiting on God* by Simone Weil; *Le Milieu Divin* by Teilhard de Chardin; *The Problem of Pain* by C. S. Lewis; *The Divine Pity* by Gerald Vann OP; and extracts from *The Autobiography of a Saint* by St Thérèse of Lisieux, translated in 1958 by Monsignor Ronald Knox.

Darton Longman and Todd Ltd for extracts from *Letters from the Desert* by Carlo Carretto, published and copyright 1972.

(Continued from Page 11)

sons." X was advised to perform more miracles, not to go to Jerusalem, and to save himself. He refused. Low rating.

Ability to Work Under Stress—"In confrontation situation, does not become rattled or confused . . . has a sense of humor when the going is difficult." X kept his cool when challenged by Scribes and Pharisees but a sense of humor was missing before Annas, Caiaphas and Pilate. Middle rating.

Ability to Communicate— ". . . few persons have difficulty understanding what he says; uses few cliches . . ." X is known for hiding the truth in parables. He defends this action with an old cliche from Isaiah about eyes that cannot see and ears that cannot hear. Low rating.

Attitude in Job—"Positive attitude toward the church and its future . . ." Some claim that in a moment of depression, X said of the church: "Behold, your house is forsaken and desolate." Others testify that he has threatened to destroy the temple. Probably he is referring to 475 Riverside Drive. Very low rating.

Interpersonal Relations— "Majority of people feel warm and positive toward person; able to relate well to those with whom he disagrees . . ." Clergy with whom he differs have been called hypocrites, blind guides, fools, and white-washed tombs. Most people have no confidence in him. He still has a few friends but no one could build a church out of them. Extremely low rating.

Completion of Tasks—". . . knows when a task has been completed in a satisfactory manner; is not a perfectionist . . ." X tells people to be perfect as their Father in heaven is perfect. Probably he does not consider any task satisfactorily completed. Low rating.

X scored more favorably on being a self-starter, skills and knowledge, productivity, creativity, and idea development. Nevertheless, the total evaluation fell far below acceptable standards for judicatory staff persons.

What is my responsibility to the evaluating process of our denomination? Should I file this report with CAS? Can I throw it away, since it was a mistake? Do I dare to question the appropriateness of the instrument?

Please send advice in a plain, brown envelope. The review form warns that personnel evaluations are "highly sensitive" and must be "treated with strict confidence." I already have taken a serious risk in revealing more than I should have about the subject.

For the Asking

- Rev. John B. McLaren, Northminster Church, 3840 Kolbe Rd., Lorain, OH 44053 has, for a fee, **Elder Development Tapes 1-5,** used only twice.
- First Church, 96 So. Monroe St., Tiffin, OH 44883 has, for the asking and shipping charges, **100 copies of "The Hymnal,"** 1933 edition.
- First Church, 409 Whitcomb Blvd., Tarpon Springs, FL 33589, has, for the asking and shipping charges, **100 copies of "The Hymnal,"** 1933 edition.
- Second Church, 410 Washington Blvd., Oak Park, IL 60302 has, for the asking and shipping charges, **200 copies of "The Hymnal,"** 1933 edition.
- First Church, P.O. Box 1503, Wickenburg, AZ 85358 has, for the asking and shipping charges, **160 copies of "The Hymnal."**

Regional Representative for Funds Development

(Synods of Southwest and Rocky Mountains)
coordinated by the United Presbyterian Foundation,
The United Presbyterian Church in the U.S.A.

Duties: Responsible for funds development for the work of the United Presbyterian Church in the U.S.A., with primary emphasis on deferred giving, bequests and wills.

Jointly represents the Synods of the Southwest, Synod of the Rocky Mountains, Division of Interpretation and Stewardship of the Support Agency, and the United Presbyterian Foundation. Accountable to and supervised by Bilateral Staff Team and Associate Director for Development of the Foundation.

Qualifications: Professional experience in fund raising, with demonstrated ability to relate to those of various views and personalities and those who seek to be responsible stewards of their wealth; membership and knowledge of the United Presbyterian Church through participation in the various organizations of the church; enthusiasm for the mission of the church; skills in public relations, including communication through verbal and written mediums; accurate; ability to keep confidences.

Travel: Extensive travel in area required.

Compensation: Annual salary: negotiable with $16,500 minimum; plus full pension benefits; one month vacation; annual study leave.

An Affirmative Action Equal Employment Opportunity Employer.

Reply to: The Rev. Donn Jann, Associate Director for Development, United Presbyterian Foundation, Room 1031, 475 Riverside Drive, New York, N.Y. 10027.

Deadline: December 1, 1975.

Statements on UPCUSA Resolution
Presented at Annual Stockholders' Meeting
of Procter & Gamble - October 13, 1975

Let us emphasize what it is this resolution asks: it is a modest proposal. It asks that our company make a study of one part of its practices—its advertising program—to see what in fact these practices communicate concerning one of the critical human issues of our time: the role of women in society. The proposal is modest—the issue is important. It is neither a simple nor a trivial matter to be concerned about issues of human dignity—and equality wherever those issues are at stake. It is part of the critical function of the church in our society to be an advocate in the struggles for human worth, seeking in its own life, and encouraging its institutional colleagues to hold up for critical scrutiny how our institutional practices further or delay the search for dignity and equality in our society.

It is to be regretted that some aspects of this resolution have lent themselves to misunderstanding and distortion. Certainly the United Presbyterian Church believes in motherhood. The United Presbyterian Church in no way de-values the role of housewife or homemaker. But vast numbers of women are neither mothers nor housewives. And millions of women who are, know that their roles of mother and homemaker do not limit or give primary definition to their lives.

What this resolution asks is that our company take more seriously what has become a critical issue in our times regarding the role of women and the attendant fundamental questions of image and identity which are being raised all over the world but with particular force in our American culture. Images—questions of identity—are terribly important. The struggles for human dignity and equality revolve around such identity questions. In our national life it was only yesterday that a Jim Crow culture—and only the day before yesterday that a slave culture—permitted and encouraged false and cruel images of millions of people—until, under what seemed to white America a most unlikely slogan and banner, that of "black is beautiful," a new day of dignity and equality was born. How quickly—overnight—our language changed. Many of those older images were forever shattered—and the issue of black and white identity moved to a significantly more mature level. Procter and Gamble has played a noteworthy role in this development.

We are involved now in another historic issue of identity concerning the role of women in our society. Harvard sociologist, Dav-

demand an investigation when $50,000 is lost in a high risk mission venture.

—People who pride themselves on airing their dirty linen in public, but who get embarrassed if anyone notices the dirt.

—People who celebrate their part in rebelling against established authority 200 years ago, but who feel that to do the same thing today is unpatriotic, blasphemous, heretical and un-presbyterian.

That's us—radical, conservative, patriotic, dissident, griping, complaining, loyal, dedicated, faithful, faithless people.

If you can laugh with me at our inconsistencies, and still pray God's forgiveness, there is hope for us to finish the revolution.

Top Executive's Job In Jeopardy

Lorrin Kreider

Pastor, First Church, Athens, Ohio

PLEASE send me your advice. I goofed, as our presbytery's Personnel Committee chairperson. My mistake could mar the reputation of an important person in our denomination. What shall I do?

The error originated as a minor oversight. Our committee decided to send key members of the presbytery an evaluation form on staff persons' performance. It was a reliable instrument, designed by the Council on Administrative Services and passed on to us with a strong recommendation from the synod's Division of Staff Services. My failure was simply this: I forgot to put the name of the person to be evaluated on one of the forms that was mailed. Because of this, one respondent made his own selection of the person he would evaluate and returned the questionnaire. The ratings are not good. They may jeopardize the position of a highly respected person. Look at them yourself.

Flexibility—"Readily adjusts plans, agenda, direction . . . supports and implements policies/programs which the person does not fully agree with . . ." X rates low. I think he would even go to the cross rather than yield.

Utilization of Other People's Ideas—". . . able to put together a program based upon the ideas/suggestions of several per-

(Continued on Page 31)

Also available in Fount Paperbacks

Journey for a Soul
GEORGE APPLETON

'Wherever you turn in this inexpensive but extraordinarily valuable paperback you will benefit from sharing this man's pilgrimage of the soul.'

Methodist Recorder

The Imitation of Christ
THOMAS A KEMPIS

After the Bible, this is perhaps the most widely read book in the world. It describes the way of the follower of Christ – an intensely practical book, which faces the temptations and difficulties of daily life, but also describes the joys and helps which are found on the way.

Autobiography of a Saint: Thérèse of Lisieux
RONALD KNOX

'Ronald Knox has bequeathed us a wholly lucid, natural and enchanting version . . . the actual process of translating seems to have vanished, and a miracle wrought, as though St Teresa were speaking to us in English . . . his triumphant gift to posterity.'

G. B. Stern, The Sunday Times

The Way of a Disciple
GEORGE APPLETON

'. . . a lovely book and an immensely rewarding one . . . his prayers have proved of help to many.'

Donald Coggan

Also available in Fount Paperbacks

BOOKS BY RITA SNOWDEN

Discoveries That Delight

'Thirty brief chapters of reflections on selected psalms . . . The book is very readable. Its style has been achieved through many years of work to produce a vehicle of religious communication with a wide appeal.'

Neville Ward, Church of England Newspaper

Further Good News

'Another enjoyable book from Rita Snowden; easy to read and with a store of good things to ponder over and store in the mind. The author shows clearly that there is much Good News in our world and that this is very much the gift of a loving God.'

Church Army Review

I Believe Here and Now

'Once again she has produced for us one of the most readable and helpful pieces of Christian witness I have seen . . .'

D. P. Munro, Life and Work

A Woman's Book of Prayer

'This book will make prayer more real and meaningful for all who use it. There is all through the book an accent of reality. Here the needs of the twentieth century are brought to God in twentieth century language.'

William Barclay

More Prayers for Women

'. . . she has that rare and valuable gift of being able to compose forms of prayer which really do express the aspirations of many people . . .'

Philip Cecil, Church Times

Fount Paperbacks

Fount is one of the leading paperback publishers of religious books and below are some of its recent titles.

- [ ] THE WAY OF ST FRANCIS Murray Bodo £2.50
- [ ] GATEWAY TO HOPE Maria Boulding £1.95
- [ ] LET PEACE DISTURB YOU Michael Buckley £1.95
- [ ] DEAR GOD, MOST OF THE TIME YOU'RE QUITE NICE Maggie Durran £1.95
- [ ] CHRISTIAN ENGLAND VOL 3 David L Edwards £4.95
- [ ] A DAZZLING DARKNESS Patrick Grant £3.95
- [ ] PRAYER AND THE PURSUIT OF HAPPINESS Richard Harries £1.95
- [ ] THE WAY OF THE CROSS Richard Holloway £1.95
- [ ] THE WOUNDED STAG William Johnston £2.50
- [ ] YES, LORD I BELIEVE Edmund Jones £1.75
- [ ] THE WORDS OF MARTIN LUTHER KING Coretta Scott King (Ed) £1.75
- [ ] BOXEN C S Lewis £4.95
- [ ] THE CASE AGAINST GOD Gerald Priestland £2.75
- [ ] A MARTYR FOR THE TRUTH Grazyna Sikorska £1.95
- [ ] PRAYERS IN LARGE PRINT Rita Snowden £2.50
- [ ] AN IMPOSSIBLE GOD Frank Topping £1.95
- [ ] WATER INTO WINE Stephen Verney £2.50

All Fount paperbacks are available at your bookshop or newsagent, or they can be ordered by post from Fount Paperbacks, Cash Sales Department, G.P.O. Box 29, Douglas, Isle of Man, British Isles. Please send purchase price, plus 15p per book, maximum postage £3. Customers outside the U.K. send purchase price, plus 15p per book. Cheque, postal or money order. No currency.

NAME (Block letters) _____

ADDRESS _____

_____

While every effort is made to keep prices low, it is sometimes necessary to increase them at short notice. Fount Paperbacks reserve the right to show new retail prices on covers which may differ from those previously advertised in the text or elsewhere.